THE HIDDEN LIGHT

By

Dr. I. V. Hilliard

Unless otherwise indicated all scriptures are from the King James Version of the Bible.

The Hidden Light
1992 Edition
Copyright by I. V. Hilliard
P. O. Box 670167
Houston, TX 77067

All rights reserved
Printed in the United States of America

ISBN 1-881357-06-6

The Hidden Light

Table of Contents

Introduction

Chapter I
The Lost Condition of Blacks
  in America.................................... 11
Character Development...................... 13
Understanding the Problem................ 15
The Resistance to Knowledge.............. 18
The Need to Know........................... 18
What is the Problem With
  Black People?................................ 20
How Beliefs Are Formed..................... 22

Chapter II
The Lostness of Black America............. 31
Parable of the Lost Coin.................... 31
Parable of the Lost Sheep................... 33
Parable of the Lost Son...................... 34
The Lost Son Who Stayed Home............ 36
The Problem of the Loss of
  Dignity and Respect........................ 41
Dispelling the Lie 43

Chapter III
Was Adam a Man of Color
  or Was Adam White?........................ 49

Chapter IV

The Biblical Origin of Black People 59
Nimrod, An Example of Dynamic Black Leadership 62
The Big Lie Told About Egypt 65
The Apostle Paul Mistaken as an Egyptian 66
Moses Mistaken for an Egyptian 67
Prejudiced Reference Books Give Illogical Reasons 68
Famous Children of Mizraim (Egypt) 68
The Philistines 69
The Land of Canaan was a Black Civilization 71
Famous Children of Canaan 72
Uriah the Hittite 72
The Black Canaanite Disciple 74
The Jebusites, the Builders of Jerusalem 75
The Black Canaanite Woman 77
Was the Black Race Cursed? 78
Melchisedec King of Salem 81
King Abimelech and Abraham 86
Ephron the Hittite 88

Chapter V

Was Jesus White or Black? 93
The Mental Chains of Slavery 94

iv

Chapter V (Continued)
*Was the Selection of the Body
    of Jesus Important?*............................ 98
*Why You Should Not Paint
    A Picture of Jesus*.............................. 102
Abraham had Two Black Wives................ 105
Keturah's Children............................. 106
Moses Married a Black Woman 106
Esau Marries Three Black Women............ 109
Should Races of People Intermarry?.......... 112
*Two Black Tribes of Israel Through
    Joseph*.. 114
*Caleb-Joshua's Friend, a Man
    of Color*.. 117

Chapter VI
*God's Strategic Use of the
    Black Man*....................................... 123
Rules for Interpretation........................ 124
*God Uses Melchizedek to Minister
    to Abraham*...................................... 125
Why is the King of Salem Black?............. 127
*Melchizedek, a Black Man, Serves
    the First Communion in Scripture*.......... 128
Abimelech Blesses Abraham................... 128
*God Uses A Black Pharoah
    to Help Israel*................................... 132
*God Uses Hobab the Midianite
    to help Moses*................................... 133

Chapter VI (Continued)
*Both Joshua and Caleb were
   Descendants of Black People*................ *136*
Was Caleb Black?................................. *136*
Was Joshua a Man of Color?.................. *138*
*The Black Woman Who Helped Save a
Nation*.. *139*
*The Black Philistine Army that
   Helped David*.................................... *142*
*The Black Man Who Rescued Jeremiah
   From Death*....................................... *143*
*Elijah Depends on the Black Woman
   to Sustain Him*................................... *146*
Joseph Hides Jesus in Black Egypt........... *149*
*The Church at Antioch With Black
   Leadership Becomes a Model*................ *151*
*The Redemption Plan is Helped
   by a Black Man*................................. *155*
*Has God Chosen Black People for
   a Purpose?*.. *156*

Chapter VII
*What America Owes the
   Black People*..................................... *163*
*Racial Controversy-
   Matter of Collaboration?* *163*
The Speech... *164*
The Debt to be Paid............................. *172*

Dedicated To...

The Members of Light Ministries - *who so freely and wonderfully accepted Biblical truths concerning people of color. Because of their willingness, obedience and faithfulness to God in support of the vision of this ministry, I had the freedom to carry out this assignment with joy.*

From the Heart Ministries - *the ministry of Dr. John and Diana Cherry, whose refreshing insight into the plight and heritage of people of color inspired the research for this book.*

And finally, My Family - *Bridget, the girls, my son-in-law and grandson. Because of their faithfulness, I had the inspiration to boldly pursue this project. Many of my dreams have become a reality because of their encouragement and support.*

The Hidden Light

Introduction

I approach the writing of this material with both a sense of destiny and caution. After careful research and study of a wide variety of material on this subject matter, I found a reservoir of information on people of color in the Bible.

The last thing I thought that was needed was another book on a subject that has been so scholarly handled by so very many. Several ministers and laymen requested my notes after hearing a series of lessons I taught on the subject of *"The Black Biblical Heritage."* At that time I began to think of the benefits of a simple, Bible-based written presentation about people of color in the Bible and their contribution in the plan of God. For the purpose of clarity in reading throughout this text, the terms "people of color" and "Black people" will be used interchangeably as they represent that particular group of people who are non-white.

This is not intended to be a secular historical presentation, but an honest interpretation of Biblical facts. There is no deliberate distortion or elimination of truth. I think we already have enough of that in much of our Christian literature.

My reason for caution is that this information would be viewed as a tool to divide believers along racial lines. My intent is quite the contrary. There is a great need among believers to understand each other and to understand the attempts of this world's system to divide us. My hope is that this book will prevent Christians from falling prey to the manipulative tactics of racism and color prejudice. These evil tactics of the world foster a mindset that will polarize and thus neutralize the Body of Christ.

My desire is that you will be enlightened by the facts that are presented and that you will rise to a new level of understanding of God's use of people of color (dark-skinned people in particular), in His plan to redeem mankind. This should cause people of color to know their importance to God and to the Body of Christ as they realize a sense of purpose and worth. Further, whites and other non-Blacks in the church who have been brainwashed by the racial prejudice that influences today's society will fully accept Blacks as a real part of the plan of God.

Much of the literature I read during the research

for this project was informative but did not present applicable principles for the daily plight of people. There are four basic objectives of this teaching:

1. <u>The Building of Self-worth and Character in Men of Color</u> - One of the main reasons for the destruction within the Black community is the lack of self-worth and low self-esteem. Over 50% of the prison population is comprised of Black people. Though Black people make up about 12% of the population of America, over 50% of the victims of murders are Black people. The lack of worth and dignity lowers the value of life among those who have no sense of worth and self-esteem.

2. <u>The Removal of the Hindrances of Black People Receiving Jesus</u> - There are alarming numbers of young Black males who are turning away from Christianity and turning to Islam. One specific reason is that they have been told the lie that the Bible is a white man's book and that nothing in it pertains to Black people. The traditional teachings of the average church, Black or white, have eliminated or overlooked the significant contributions of Black people in the plan of God. The information contained in this book will dispel the lie that the Bible is a white man's book. You will discover, as I did,

that the Bible is a book about people of all colors and color was not a factor.

3. <u>The Ministry to the Uncovering of the Prejudice Attitude in the Church</u> - The prejudice attitude in the Christian church is an area that nobody wants to address, but it needs some immediate attention. It is a fact that there will always be prejudice in the world's system, but it should not be so in the Church. Jesus taught that the Church should be the example to the world in Matthew 5:13-17.

"Ye are the salt of the earth: but if the salt have lost his savour, wherewith shall it be salted? It is thenceforth good for nothing, but to be cast out, and to be trodden under foot of men. Ye are the light of the world. A city that is set on a hill cannot be hid."

It appears that many white Christians have been negatively influenced by the media's misrepresentation of people of color (Black people in particular). This has produced an accepted level of color prejudice that has gone unaddressed by the white clergy. Sunday is the most segregated day in America. On a large scale the different races and colors of people congregate together with the subtle exclusion of the other races. Remember, either we (the church) are the salt of the earth or we are good for nothing. Unfortunately, many in the church on both sides of the issue are in a state of denial relative to this problem. If left undealt with, there will never be an attempt to understand each other.

4. <u>To Inform the Reader About the Contributions that People of Color Have Made to the Plan of God.</u> - The information that is included in this book is not unknown by Bible scholars, but simply untaught. The willful elimination of this kind of information in Christian circles has added to the development of the poor self-esteem of people of color. The accurate portrayal of Biblical characters based on their clearly revealed heritage will demonstrate God's use of Black people in His wonderful plan to redeem mankind.

As you absorb the material in the following pages, I trust that this presentation will not be the sum total of your research effort to know the truth. This work is intended to whet your appetite for learning and knowing the role that men and women of color play in the Bible.

CHAPTER I

The Lost Condition of Blacks in America

CHAPTER I

The Lost Condition of Blacks in America

There are some very astounding statistics that spurred me into studying the socio-spiritual condition of the Black male in America. The Black male is almost a candidiate for the endangered species list. An endangered species is classified as a species that is becoming extinct. The **"Black Male"** in America is in serious trouble and if the tide is not turned quickly the end results will be devastating.

Blacks make up about 12% of the population in America which is the reason we are classified as minorities. Many have associated the word minority as synonymous with inferiority. Minority has to do with a numerical comparison and not with the quality of character or worth of an individual.

Here is the shocking information on this 12% of the population of America. Over 50% of the prison population is made of Black people. Greater than 50% of the murder victims in this country are Black people. There are more Black baby boys born than baby girls, but by the time a young Black woman reaches adulthood, she outnumbers her available Black male counterparts six to one. You must agree that these are alarming statistics. The tragic part is that conditions are not getting any better, but in reality, are getting worse by the day.

We have a very serious problem that will not disappear by denying its existence. If the Black man was a bird in the wild, he would probably be placed on the endangered species list, and millions of dollars would be allocated to reverse the plight of his extinction. True enough, the problem that exists is not the cause of some present broad-scale, open, overt act of government. Many of the Blacks who are incarcerated actually disobeyed the law and were legally convicted and properly (in most cases) sentenced per the statutes of the law. The problems of hopelessness, violence and despair exist because of the subtle acceptable racial prejudice that still exists in America. When people are robbed of the knowledge of who they are and are treated as second class inferior beings, it grossly affects their behavior.

Further, much of the crime, including the homicides, in the Black community is Black-on

-Black crime. Where does the responsibility for all of this misbehavior lie? Why are so many Black people seemingly so bent on a path of self-destruction? What is the reason for this widespread misbehavior? What is the cause of this character flaw which seems to lower the appreciation of the value of a life?

Character Development

It all goes back to the way one's character is developed. Character is behavior on display and is the visible demonstration of a person's deep-seated beliefs and values. Character is not a product of the new birth experience but must be shaped and developed to conform with the character exhibited by the Lord Jesus Christ. The following passage in the Book of Romans clearly shows this to be the case.

"I beseech you therefore, brethren, by the mercies of God, that ye present your bodies a living sacrifice, holy, acceptable unto God, which is your reasonable service. And be not conformed to this world: but be ye transformed by the renewing of your mind, that ye may prove what is that good, and acceptable, and perfect, will of God." Romans 12:1-2

Thus, the reason many Christians commit

crimes, misbehave, are violent, are prejudiced, are cold, and are indifferent is because they have not renewed their thinking and developed their character.

There are four essential elements of Godly character. These four elements are: commitment, integrity, heritage, and discipline. One of the problems that the Black man faces is a lack of understanding of who he is, where he came from, and what has been his contribution to his environment. This is in essence the study of his heritage.

It is difficult for the average person to understand why not knowing one's contribution or the sense of how not making a contribution can affect one's behavior. Yet, this same mind-set is the cause of many broken marriages and relationships. We all have several basic psychological needs that contribute to a sense of worth and dignity. We have a need to be needed, a need to be wanted, and a need to have purpose. When a marriage partner feels that they are not valued in the marriage or that they are not needed, wanted or have purpose, their behavior toward the other partner is affected.

When a marriage partner feels that he or she has not made a contribution to the marriage, that person most likely assumes an inferior role in the relationship. So it is with people of color in this society, because there is a feeling of not having made a contribution to this world, many Blacks assume a role of thinking inferior, and acting inferior. The real tragedy is that this belief of not having made a contribution is untrue, but simply the knowledge of what that contribution has been is unknown.

Our approach to this issue will be strictly from a Biblical perspective to show the diabolical exclusion of information relative to the Black man's Biblical heritage. It is understandable why this was done in the Euro-centric American system; it helped to perpetuate slavery and justify its existence by degrading Black people (people of color) to a sub-human role. The church, however, is the God-ordained protector and steward of truth and should not participate in any way in obscuring truth.

Understanding the Problem

If I do not know who I am or the truth about where I came from, it is difficult to know and understand my purpose for being.

If I do not know my purpose, I cannot act according to that purpose which I do not know.

I will undoubtedly behave outside of my intended created purpose which will be *"misbehavior"*. The extent of this misbehavior will determine how the society I live in responds to me and how I will react to it.

Behavior is changed by purposeful, calculated effort based on new information. By new information I do not mean a recent contemporary thought process but information that is new to the recipient. This information may be or may not be solely historical in nature. Because the Black man has not known the information relative to his heritage, his behavior has been severely affected.

Many Blacks are incapable of behaving like the proud, integrity-filled heritage from which they descended because the knowledge of this heritage has been replaced by lies about their past that are disgraceful and humiliating.

Thousands upon thousands of Blacks in America suffer from a lack of self-worth, a poor self-esteem, poor self-image and thus a poor appreciation of others (Black people) who look like them. This condition has minimized the desire to achieve and pursue a better life. The Bible teaches that a people can be destroyed for a lack of knowledge. *"My people are destroyed for a lack of knowledge..."* Hosea 4:6

What is knowledge? Knowledge is information about a past event, experience, or happening. So the scripture is saying that destruction follows a people who have no information of past experiences, events and happenings. Heritage by definition is the knowledge of culture, characteristics, and behavior that is passed down from one's ancestors. Heritage is an essential component for the development of positive behavior, positive self image and a deterrent to destruction!

The Black man in America and other parts of the world has been denied proper access to the knowledge of his past ancestors. The white American educational system has for the most part eliminated or distorted this information. The social system in which the Black man lives has influenced him to think that a pursuit of Black heritage information is tantamount to civil rebellion. The Church, the only vestige of truth and moral conscience of the world, has been silent and all but aligned itself with the rhythm of prejudice in the world.

This writing touches an area that is certainly not unknown, just simply untaught by traditional church scholars or pulpiteers. Sure, it genders some criticism, but so did the message of those prophets and teachers in the Bible who touched on the traditionally untouched issues and provoked people to think.

The Resistance to Knowledge

I remember very vividly how I encountered resistance to this teaching when I first began to share this in our local church which is made up of mostly Black people. The main reason for the original resistance is the dominant influence of this society on our thinking. Blacks have been passively trained and taught to ignore their history, their contribution, and to speak out against the status quo is to be a troublemaker.

Knowing this, I approached the teaching in our local church very tactfully, allowing time to break down the barriers of resistance in order to strategically bombard the minds and hearts of the people with the spiritual truths that would bring freedom and self-worth.

The Need To Know

The Bible is filled with many exciting truths that will transform the lives of people. We are suffering in this society from years of divisions and strife between races and people of different skin colors. People have a desire to change, to live together, to throw off the garments of prejudice, but lack the knowledge of how it is to be done.

The reason for the upsurge of violence in our cities and the resurfacing of the racial tensions is due to the great misunderstandings people have about each other. The broad spread of destructive negative stereotypes that people have of each other prohibits cooperation among people who verbally express a desire to cooperate and work together.

The problem is compounded as you look at the race relations in the Church body nationwide. The inequities are easily seen. The Church, according to Jesus, is to be the light to the world and the salt of the earth. In other words (in this context) the Church should be the example to the world of how people of different races and backgrounds should get along. Unfortunately, the same misconceptions that people had about those of other races, before their new birth experience, are not eradicated at the new birth. These false beliefs and prejudices must be dealt with through the process of the renewing of the mind. Unfortunately, many Christians have never dealt with these ingrained prejudices.

The Black man/white man controversy is almost as old as this nation. A significant key to our understanding and respecting each other, Black and white, can be based on the truths revealed in the Word of God. Biblical information is in a category all its own. The majority of the Christian world accepts its authenticity, and will not question it as "the" standard of righteousness. When people are presented with information about the Black man from God's perspective and see the Black man functioning with authority, integrity and power in an arena that is accepted as the standard of righteousness, the walls of prejudice and racism will begin to crumble and ultimately fall.

This book will not change the racial climate in the unsaved world, although I believe it will have some effect on the unsaved population. I do trust that as the racial climate in the body of Christ is transformed from one of tolerance of non-white people to one of full acceptance, it could impact and influence the climate of the nation.

What is the Problem with Black People?

People on both sides of the color fence are asking this question without receiving a clear distinct answer. Black people find it difficult to explain to other races and people why they are having the problems they are experiencing within the Black community. Whites are frustrated because they find it difficult to empathize with conditions and mental attitudes that are the results of years of enslavement and second class citizenship.

This study will shed light on the great misunderstanding and communication rift between two powerful groups of people in America. It is interesting to note that color is not a major factor in the civilizations of the past and particularly in the days of Biblical culture. However, both Christians and non-Christians in America know that the color of one's skin is a major factor by which people are judged. It is then hypocritical to say that "you don't see color". We all see color and have been trained in this culture to associate certain attitudes and stereotypes with the color of a person's skin and the race to which he belongs.

The mass media is the generator of the cultural signals that give direction of thought to this society. There has been a clear negative portrayal of Black people in the mass media. This overall negative message about the character of blacks that is shown in news clips and on the silver screen far outweighs those positive role models of Black sports figures, entertainers and politicians. America has drawn clear distinct lines of the judgement of worth, of potential, and of character on the basis of the color of skin.

This judgmental process is unfair and can be destructive, especially when judgments are made based on misinformation from the indoctrination of a society that has thrived on prejudices and racism. The non-Black Christians should not become a party to this racially prejudiced thinking, but must renew their minds to remove the false stereotypes imposed on them by this culture. The information contained in the following pages will provide the necessary enlightenment to convince the believer to cast down the indoctrinations of this world and bring into captivity his thoughts to the obedience of Christ.

"Casting down imaginations, and every high thing that exalteth itself against the knowledge of God, and bringing into captivity every thought to the obedience of Christ;" II Corinthians 10:5

How Beliefs are Formed

Beliefs are formed at a very early age and normally are the product of information received from one's environment. If that information is incorrect and the propaganda of a racist society, the thinking of a person can be misdirected. This misdirection of thought has occurred in both Black and white communities. The Black man has been deprived of information about his past and is therefore dependent on the interpretation that others give him about himself to develop a sense of worth and dignity. Many white brothers and sisters in the Body of Christ have grown up in a culture that has indoctrinated them with a superior attitude concerning themselves and the inferior role others (Blacks in particular) should have in "their" world.

Racist indoctrination is never as blatant as a white parent aggressively and intentionally brainwashing or talking to their children day after day about the inferiority of Black people. It is done much more subtly, yet in very potent ways. As the child observes the adult's world reaction toward Black people, his attitude is shaped, and his beliefs are formed.

Racist propaganda is spread in many cities daily through the newscasts that place an over-emphasis on crimes that **"Black Men"** commit in their lead stories. This sends a strong message to the community that only Blacks are misbehaving and should be feared and avoided.

Idle words and racial jokes mentioned around young pliable minds tend to foster a certain attitude toward a certain race and color of people. Thus, feelings of superiority or inferiority are shaped during the innocence of childhood.

This attitude is visible in the Church by the disproportionate roles of leadership assigned to Black Christians who attend in large numbers churches with white leadership. These churches are not shining examples that the prejudice issue has been overcome. Blacks have always longed to be a part of white institutions, colleges, schools, and country clubs because there is the misconception of that which is white is better. **There is a false sense of worth felt by Blacks when the whites accept them into their group.** You cannot point to all white churches with Blacks who attend as the example of the absence of racism. The real acid test of the eradication of prejudice among White/Black Christians occurs when there are proportionate leadership roles and when there are white Christians following Black leadership in the Church. It is sad to say that in this area it appears that the unsaved world has made more progress than the Body of Christ.

The Black people are suffering from years of

inferior treatment and dehumanizing tactics that have robbed them of their dignity, their self esteem, their self-worth and self-respect. This inferior mindset is at the the root of the problems that Blacks create for themselves. Think about it. Although only 12% of the population of this country is Black people (Afro-American descent), more than 50% of the prison population is made up of Black people. The next tragic statistic is that at this writing, in 50% of all the homicides in the nation the victims are Black people. It would take a blind, dishonest person to say that those numbers are not gravely disproportionate to the overall population of our nation.

Why are Black people acting so out of step with what is expected and accepted in this society? Are they incapable of conforming to a civilized society's standards? What's the problem? Why are we killing each other by the thousands? Why are so many young Blacks in jail? Why is it that a young Black male is more likely to be killed by a youthful counterpart than by some dreaded disease before he reaches age 25?

The problem stems from the understanding of who you are, what your purpose is, and what contributions your kind has made to this world. It may be difficult for my non-Black readers to understand this point, but stick with me and you will see what I mean. **An inferiority complex will stagnate one's pursuit to achieve.** This is readily seen in the story of the children of Israel at Kadesh Barnea.

"But the men that went up with him said, We be not able to go up against the people; for they are stronger than we."

"And they brought up an evil report of the land which they had searched unto the children of Israel, saying, The land, through which we have gone to search it, is a land that eateth up the inhabitants thereof; and all the people that we saw in it are men of a great stature."

"And there we saw the giants, the sons of Anak, which come of the giants: and we were in our own sight as grasshoppers, and so we were in their sight." Numbers 13:31-33

Ten of the spies saw themselves inferior to the inhabitants of the promised land and thought that the inhabitants saw the children of Israel as being inferior also. This was far from the truth, but this inferiority complex totally paralyzed the adult Israeli nation and deprived them of the privileges of their new freedom.

There has been an assault on the dignity of people of color in this nation that the past years of government incentive programs could not restore. The creation of a handout mentality through an ill-designed welfare system is the result of the misconception of what this nation really owes the Black people. It also creates an inferior image to the Black man about his ability to achieve in this society. Proper restitution is not a hand-out alone, but the restoration of the dignity and worth of the individual which places him mentally on the same economic playing field with others.

Once American Christians, both Blacks and whites, get a clear understanding about the Black man from a Biblical perspective, the Christian Church will be transformed. The time is now, and because you have read this far I know that you are a serious seeker, and this part of your search will not be in vain. Once we are exposed to the truth of the Word of God on His purpose, use, and relationship with people of color, we will have sufficient information from this unquestionable reference source to correct our thinking. Once our thinking is properly affected, then our attitudes and behavior will change toward each other.

We are about to embark on a journey through

the scriptures that will revolutionize your thinking and how you will read the Bible from this time forth. The information that I will share with you is not something that is unknown, but it is critical information that is untaught. I have watched this information transform men and women both Black and white, and I have witnessed it transform Pastors and their churches. Prepare yourself for an excursion through the scriptures that will bring a refreshing, enlightening view of the people of color.

CHAPTER II

The Lostness of Black America

CHAPTER II

The Lostness of Black America

Jesus implied that when a person or a thing is lost, it demands immediate attention to bring it to a place of recovery. The parable recorded in the gospel of Luke, the 15th Chapter, fully expresses allegorically the various states of a type of lostness seen in Black people in America.

Parable of the Lost Coin

"Either what woman having ten pieces of silver, if she lose one piece, doth not light a candle, and sweep the house, and seek diligently till she find it?"

"And when she hath found it, she calleth her friends and her neighbours together, saying, Rejoice with me; for I have found the piece which I had lost."

"Likewise, I say unto you, there is joy in the presence of the angels of God over one sinner that repenteth." Luke 15:8-10

Several factors must be addressed as we examine this parable: **nothing gets lost of its own accord, and the state of lostness can never be recovered** without proper assistance. Look at the lost coin. This represents that segment of this Black generation that is lost from fulfilling its purpose. Because the purpose for being has never been defined, it is difficult for people of color to plot a course for their future. Therefore, I will only meander along in life, tossed about by the waves of the current political administration and every wave of economic turmoil and educational mishap.

The image of successful Blacks which automatically becomes the goal of young Blacks has been distorted by the media.

Unfortunately, the average Black child feels that he has a better chance at becoming an entertainer or an athlete than he does at other professions. This is definitely a case of misguided and misdirected ambitions. This is an unrealistic expectation and at most is a short-lived experience. Yes, some Blacks will become successful athletes and entertainers and will receive lucrative contracts, but most will not. A proper road map must be given so that in the pursuit of success, masses of young Blacks will not become lost in this economic wilderness. If a person is not instructed about his potential to achieve, that person will most likely be a low achiever. The story of the lost coin best illustrates a thing that maintains its potential worth on the open market, but cannot fulfill that potential until it has been recovered and released. Much talent and brilliance is housed in people of color who live a life in a "less than God's will" situation, mainly because of unfulfilled purpose.

Parable of the Lost Sheep

"And he spake this parable unto them, saying,"

"What man of you, having an hundred sheep, if he lose one of them, doth not leave the ninety and nine in the wilderness, and go after that which is lost, until he find it?"

"And when he hath found it, he layeth it on his shoulders, rejoicing."

"And when he cometh home, he calleth together his friends and neighbours, saying unto them, Rejoice with me; for I have found my sheep which was lost."

"I say unto you, that likewise joy shall be in heaven over one sinner that repenteth, more than over ninety and nine just persons, which need no repentance." Luke 15:3-7

Many Blacks in this society are lost like the sheep in the parable, in that they are devoid of proper direction. This absence of direction is due to those who are in leadership positions not providing enough structure, directions, or sign posts to assist other Blacks in staying on course with their lives. This is the reason young Black men want to sell drugs and get involved in economic crimes because there is a misdirection of worth and success! Many young Blacks believe worth is in what you have and, therefore, you must **"get"** no matter the cost. This misguided search for worth has blinded thousands of young Blacks in America who, like the sheep, nibble themselves away from the mainstream of society and begin to function outside of the law.

Parable of the Lost Son

"And He said, A certain man had two sons:"

"And the younger of them said to his father, Father, give me the portion of goods that falleth to me. And he divided unto them his living."

"And not many days after the younger son gathered all together, and took his journey into a far country, and there wasted his substance with riotous living."

"And when he had spent all, there arose a mighty famine in that land; and he began to be in want."

"And he went and joined himself to a citizen of that country; and he sent him into his fields to feed swine."

"And he would fain have filled his belly with the husks that the swine did eat: and no man gave unto him."

"And when he came to himself, he said, How many hired servants of my father's have bread enough and to spare, and I perish with hunger!"

"I will arise and go to my father, and will say unto him, Father, I have sinned against heaven, and before thee,"

"And am no more worthy to be called thy son: make me as one of thy hired servants."

"And he arose, and came to his father. But when he was yet a great way off, his father saw him, and had compassion, and ran, and fell on his neck, and kissed him." Luke 15:11-20

Then there are those Blacks who are lost like the prodigal son, in that they have disrespected authority and are suffering the consequences of the hogpen of incarceration. The breakdown of the family value system begins with a disrespect for the leadership and authority in the home. This disrespect bleeds over into every area of the person's life and meets with devastating consequences when the laws of society are violated. The prisons are filled with Black men and women because there was a disrespect for authority (the laws of government), and because they lacked the proper economic clout to make proper representation in a court of law, they received the maximum punishment for their crimes.

The Lost Son Who Stayed Home

"Now his elder son was in the field: and as he came and drew nigh to the house, he heard musick and dancing."

"And he called one of the servants, and asked what these things meant."

"And he said unto him, Thy brother is come; and thy father hath killed the fatted calf, because he hath received him safe and sound."

"And he was angry, and would not go in: therefore came his father out, and intreated

him."

"And he answering said to his father, Lo, these many years do I serve thee, neither transgressed I at any time thy commandment: and yet thou never gavest me a kid, that I might make merry with my friends:"

"But as soon as this thy son was come, which hath devoured thy living with harlots, thou hast killed for him the fatted calf."

"And he said unto him, Son, thou art ever with me, and all that I have is thine."

"It was meet that we should make merry, and be glad: for this thy brother was dead, and is alive again; and was lost, and is found." Luke 15:25-32

Finally, there are those elite Blacks who are lost in the similitude of the elder brother who stayed home and out of trouble. His condition of lostness was in that he thought his disrespect for and improper relationship with his recovering brother were justifiable. This elder brother represents that class of the Black professionals who attempt to disassociate themselves from their Black brothers and sisters because they have made the Euro-centric system work for them. These Blacks can easily be identified because they ardently show their intolerance with the struggles most Blacks are having. They enjoy being able to say that they were the only ones (Black persons) at the company's Annual Christmas Party, or the only one who works for a certain company.

There is a false sense of worth because they are being tolerated by the whites they admire. This condition of lostness, like that of the prodigal's brother, is difficult to come to grips with because of the self-righteous, self-justification and prideful attitudes they justify by their success.

Again, I must mention that this is the condition of many Black Christians who attend mostly white congregations. There is the sense that because a white person has allowed them to be a part of their institutions, they have arrived at a certain level in life that makes them have worth. This is much like the same desire that Blacks have in the world to be accepted so that they can have the feeling of worth.

Now this is not a put-down, but just an observation. This is a misguided sense of worth built on the decision of another person's acceptance. **The only valid sense of worth is that** worth that comes from knowing who you are from God's perspective and knowing you are accepted unconditionally by God.

Many of you who are reading this book will initially have a difficult time accepting what I am saying unless a white Christian organization or white renown minister agrees with me. I am not saying that anything written by anybody should be swallowed hook, line, and sinker without some scrutiny. However, **this society has an unspoken law that what a Black man does is not worth much unless a white man says its okay.**

I am often asked how many white people attend my church, as though the over 3,000 Black membership (at this writing) is not significant unless some whites are members. It is that same way in business. Black businessmen are asked how many white clients they have, as though it takes white clients to be called successful.

This kind of thinking has caused many successful Blacks to seek white acceptance and accreditation for what they do to the abandonment of the proper relationship and fellowship with their Black brothers and sisters. It is awesome that the Orientals will stick together and work together for their community's good. Jews are known worldwide for their allegiance to each other. Every race of people has a track record of cooperation among themselves to improve their conditions, except Blacks. This is a serious condition of lostness when we as Black people choose to forsake each other to be tolerated, temporarily, by others.

Jesus said on many occasions that he was assigned to seek and to save that which was lost. This lostness that Jesus talked about referred to those who were without eternal life, but yet not limited to eternal life. The salvation that Jesus gives brings wholeness to life. It brings a unique quality of living to life.

"The thief cometh not, but for to steal, and to kill, and to destroy: I am come that they might have life, and that they might have it more abundantly." John 10:10"

You and I must see ourselves as witnesses to bring the salvation message to the world, but moreover we are responsible for sharing a wholeness of life with fellow brothers and sisters. Prejudice, stereotypes, and racial fears robbed you of this God kind of life.

It was the example of Jesus to address the needs of those who were in a "less than God's will" position in life. If the Church is to follow the example of Jesus, we must assist the people of color in this nation in a complete recovery process from these aforementioned conditions of lostness. Remember, nothing that is lost can find its way. It cannot be recovered without some assistance.

Have you ever been traveling cross-country and made a wrong turn and discovered that you were lost? Either the assistance of a person or a road sign or a road map gave you the information to make the necessary adjustments to get back on course. I present to you that it is the proper interpretation of the Word of God on several key issues relative to the origin and worth of the Black man to God that will provide both Black and white with the mid-course adjustment to get on a wholesome course of unity in the Body of Christ. This knowledge will set the minds of Blacks and whites free from the indoctrinations of the slavery era that has led to mistrust, inferior and superior feelings, especially among the Christians in the Church.

The Problem of the Loss of Dignity and Respect

We have discussed earlier that when a man has lost his sense of dignity, self-respect and self-worth, his behavior is negatively influenced. The dictionary defines worth as "the esteem in which a person or a thing is held". Most people derive their self-esteem from the opinions of others. If people have been misinformed, then their opinions will be affected and will give birth to an erroneous assessment of the worth of an individual(s).

Instinctively, you derive a sense of worth from the information that you receive about yourself from others in your sphere of influence. It is true that the history of the Black man has been grossly misrepresented here in this country. The objective of the slave owners was to do as much as possible to keep the slaves ignorant of their past and ignorant of their potential in order to keep them enslaved. Slaves were prohibited from learning to read, because reading gives birth to knowledge and knowledge elevates.

Just recently, in some of the history books to be used in the educational system of this nation, over 200 errors were cited in reference to the Euro-American history. It is no wonder that Euro-Centric scholars have extreme difficulty addressing the history of Black-skinned people. The history book we will use as our text will be the Bible. I believe that the greatest threat to the slave owners was not so much the reading of the Euro-centric view of history which could be (was) distorted to eliminate the contributions of the Black-skinned people, but the reading of the Bible which contains an even more potent reservoir of self-esteem building information for people of color.

Dispelling the Lie

If you knew of a lie that was being told that was robbing a man of the knowledge of Jesus, would you tell him the truth so that he could experience salvation?

Sure you would, if you are a real Christian! It has been proven in numerous secular texts that the contributions of people of color have been eliminated to achieve some misguided end by misguided men. The Church cannot afford to be numbered among those who withhold the truth. Sadly to say, **the Christian world is guilty of the same fraudulent accounts the secular historians have made by ignoring the contributions of the men and women of color who participated in the plan of God.**

The first defense against the previous indictment which will rise from the ranks of good-hearted, well-meaning white Christian churches will be: God is not a respecter of persons and He uses whomever He will. This is said as if to imply that it does not matter to them what color a person is and it is alright until you tell them Jesus was probably a Black man. The next thought process is to attack the mere mentioning of an error in Christian literature, a gross error, could occur. Out of their loving hearts they will say color doesn't matter. Of course no defense is good without supportive witnesses, so they will find some Black persons who have disassociated themselves from their Black brothers and sisters who will agree that the color issue really doesn't matter. I will agree on all points. The color of a person does not matter and is insignificant with God.

However it would be distortion of truth and a misrepresentation to tell a man life's story and attach another person's picture to his biography. If this happens in a local newspaper, there would be community outrage. So it does matter how truth, even secular truth, is told.

The truth is that it also matters how the truth of the Word of God is presented. If a person has Black skin and he is painted with white skin in the Bible story books, that is a gross misrepresentation of the truth. The world winks at it but the Church world cannot tolerate such blatant misrepresentations. It was this kind of tactic that the prejudiced world system has used to eliminate the contributions of the Black people to the civilized world, thus promoting inferiority and low self-esteem. We must be careful so that this does not happen as we handle the Word of God and the story of redemption. Remember, we must give an account for our stewardship of the truth.

CHAPTER III

Was Adam a Man of Color or Was Adam White?

CHAPTER III

Was Adam a Man of Color or Was Adam White?

There is a scripture in Titus 3:9 and a companion scripture in I Timothy 1:4 that warns the believer to avoid aimless studies in genealogy.

"But avoid foolish questions, and genealogies, and contentions, and strivings about the law; for they are unprofitable and vain." Titus 3:9

"Neither give heed to fables and endless genealogies, which minister questions, rather than godly edifying which is in faith: so do." I Timothy 1:4

This will not be an aimless study in genealogy because we have clear-cut goals and four major objectives. They are:

1. To build the self-image and character of the people of color,

2. To address the prejudice issue in the Body of Christ,

3. To remove the hindrances of many

young Blacks receiving Christ as their saviour, and

    4. To provide much needed information to the Body of Christ about the contributions of Blacks in the plan of God.

Let's begin with the story of Noah's children after the flood.

"Now these are the generations of the sons of Noah, Shem, Ham, and Japheth: and unto them were sons born after the flood." Gen 10:1

"And the sons of Ham; Cush, and Mizraim, and Phut, and Canaan. And the sons of Cush; Seba, and Havilah, and Sabtah, and Raamah, and Sabtechah: ...." Gen. 10:6-7

This story takes place following the great earth-destroying, transforming deluge. The Bible records that only Noah and his sons and their families survived the flood. Thus, the repopulation of the earth and division of the nations of people that we see today came from Noah and his sons. So, the origin of the nations is found in the genealogy of Noah's sons.

Please note that the majority of Biblical scholars agree that Ham was a black son of Noah. If Ham was Black, then all of his offsprings were also dark or black-skinned people. One of Ham's grandsons was Havilah for whom the area of land he settled was named. So when we see the phrase "land of Havilah" it is referencing the land inhabited by Havilah, the dark-skinned son of Ham and his offsprings who were also dark-skinned people of color.

The Hebrew name **"Mizraim"** is in other places translated **"Egypt"** and the name **"Cush"** is in other places translated **"Ethiopia."** Using just a little knowledge of eastern geography will reveal that Egypt and Ethiopia are in Africa which is still mostly inhabited by dark-skinned people.

In Genesis, chapter two and verse seven, we see further reference to this **land of Havilah**.

"And the Lord God formed man of the dust of the ground, and breathed into his nostrils the breath of life; and man became a living soul.

And the Lord God planted a garden eastward in Eden; and there he put the man whom he had formed.

And out of the ground made the Lord God to grow every tree that is pleasant to the sight, and good for food; the tree of life also in the midst of the garden, and the tree of knowledge of good and evil.

And a river went out of Eden to water the garden; and from thence it was parted and became into four heads.

The name of the first is Pison: that is it which compasseth <u>the whole land of Havilah</u>. where there is gold;

And the gold of that land is good: there is bdellium and the onyx stone.

And the name of the second river is Gihon: the same is it that compasseth <u>the whole land of Ethiopia</u>.

And the name of the third river is Hiddekel: that is it which goeth toward the east of Assyria. And the fourth river is Euphrates.

And the Lord God took the man, and put him into the garden of Eden to dress it and to keep it. Genesis 2:7-15

In this passage, it is amazing to discover that the garden of Eden is geographically located in the land that was inhabited and no doubt named for two of Ham's (black-skinned Ham) sons, Havilah and Cush (Ethiopia). It is safe to say that the garden of Eden, where Adam was placed, was located on the continent of Africa. Further, the river Gihon is also known as the Nile river, which is located in Africa.

The meaning of Adam's name in the Hebrew tongue is dark or red earth. It is a sure thing that Adam, being made from dirt in the heart of Africa, was not made a white man. This would be most inconsistent with the character of God who does all things well, since it is widely known that a light-skinned person would have an extremely difficult time surviving in the climate of Africa.

Undoubtedly, Adam was a man of color, and he was the first Biblical representation of the human race. Only a few years ago, a group of notable scientists proved that based on certain genetic facts, the mother of all creation was a black-skinned woman. This article appeared on the front cover of Newsweek Magazine in the September 23, 1991, issue and a similar article appeared in U. S. News & World Report in the September 16, 1991 issue.

God created a world that was perfect in every way and said that it was good. He made Adam a man of color from the dirt of the ground and said of man that he was good. So then the truth of the matter is that the people of color are not an inferior after thought of God but were a real part of the plan of God. To this dark-skinned Black man, God gave dominion over the earth to care for it, to subdue it, and endowed him with the intellectual brilliance to name all the animals and to manage His creation.

After first hearing this, many Blacks experience a true feeling of self-respect and self-worth. You see, most people, Blacks and whites, think that God made all white people and was going on with his plan when the Black man interrupted things by appearing unannounced on the scene. When the truth of the matter (as revealed through the scripture), is that God made Adam a man of color and not white.

There should be no need for Blacks feeling superior to whites, in that the fall of mankind was a shortcoming of these two people of color in Africa (Adam and Eve) to obey the expressed will of God. It is only through the second

Adam, Jesus the Christ, that all men are able to live a fulfilled life. This is the truth that must be told!

CHAPTER IV

The Biblical Origin of the Black People

CHAPTER IV

The Biblical Origin of the Black People

The Biblical story of the repopulation of the world after the great flood holds the key to the different nations and races of people. Genesis 10:1,6-20 records the descendants of Noah's Black son Ham, who is widely accepted as the father of the races of people of color. The origin of the various races of dark-skinned people can be traced back to one of Ham's sons. Because the emphasis of the book is to dispel the notion that <u>the color of a person's skin renders him or her an inferior being,</u> we will not address the various races of these black-skinned people but simply highlight their Black heritage.

"Now these are the generations of the sons of Noah, Shem, Ham, and Japheth: and unto them were sons born after the flood." Genesis 10:1

"And the sons of Ham; Cush, and Mizraim, and Phut, and Canaan."

"And the sons of Cush; Seba, and Havilah, and Sabtah, and Raamah, and Sabtechah: and the sons of Raamah; Sheba, and Dedan."

"And Cush begat Nimrod: he began to be a

mighty one in the earth."

"He was a mighty hunter before the Lord: wherefore it is said, Even as Nimrod the mighty hunter before the Lord."

"And the beginning of his kingdom was <u>Babel</u>, and Erech, and Accad, and Calneh, in the land of Shinar."

"Out of that land went forth Asshur, and builded <u>Nineveh</u>, and the city Rehoboth, and Calah,"

"And Resen between Nineveh and Calah: the same is a great city."

"And Mizraim begat Ludim, and Anamim, and Lehabim, and Naphtuhim,"

"And Pathrusim, and Casluhim, (out of whom came <u>Philistim</u>,) and Caphtorim."

"And Canaan begat <u>Sidon</u> his firstborn, and <u>Heth</u>," (The Father of the Hittites)

"And the <u>Jebusite</u>, and the <u>Amorite</u>, and the <u>Girgasite</u>,"

"And the <u>Hivite</u>, and the Arkite, and the Sinite,"
"And the Arvadite, and the Zemarite, and the

Hamathite: and afterward were the families of the <u>Canaanites</u> spread abroad."

"And the border of the Canaanites was from <u>Sidon</u>, as thou comest to Gerar, unto <u>Gaza</u>; as thou goest, unto <u>Sodom</u>, and <u>Gomorrah</u>, and Admah, and Zeboim, even unto Lasha."

"These are the sons of Ham, after their families, after their tongues, in their countries, and in their nations." Genesis 10:6-20

I have made several notations in the previous text to highlight some familiar Biblical nations of people that are portrayed in films and Bible storybooks as being white, when in fact these were black people, descendants of Black Ham. This was an eye-opening revelation, to know that many nations that I thought all my life were white were really Black. This error in thinking occurred because of the way the Bible was taught and pictured in this society. Although portrayed in the Bible storybooks as white, these nations were not white but were really proud prosperous nations of Black people.

The Bible is not a book all about the Jews (who are also incorrectly portrayed as being an all white-skinned nation of people). The Bible story books portray the story of mostly white characters with other people of color playing only secondary, insignificant roles every now and then.

Nimrod: An Example of Dynamic Black Leadership

"And the whole earth was of one language, and of one speech."

"And it came to pass, as they journeyed from the east, that they found a plain in the land of Shinar; and they dwelt there."

"And they said one to another, Go to, let us make brick, and burn them thoroughly. And they had brick for stone, and slime had they for mortar."

"And they said, Go to, let us build us a city and a tower, whose top may reach unto heaven; and let us make us a name, lest we be scattered abroad upon the face of the whole earth."

"And the Lord came down to see the city and the tower, which the children of men builded."

"And the Lord said, Behold, the people is one, and they have all one language; and this they begin to do: and now nothing will be restrained

from them, which they have imagined to do."

"Go to, let us go down, and there confound their language, that they may not understand one another's speech."

"So the Lord scattered them abroad from thence upon the face of all the earth: and they left off to build the city."

"Therefore is the name of it called Babel; because the Lord did there confound the language of all the earth: and from thence did the Lord scatter them abroad upon the face of all the earth." Genesis 11:1-9

It amazes me that out of all of the pictures I have seen and stories that I have heard about the building of the tower of Babel that there is not the slightest mentioning that Nimrod was a Black man. Nimrod was the son of Cush (Ethiopia). He was, in reality, a Black Ethiopian who was a mighty hunter before the Lord and led the whole world. Critics will probably jump in immediately and say that he was misleading the nations against God, so that discredits him from a stature of greatness.

Nimrod, like King David and King Solomon, made mistakes, but that does not discredit the genius and leadership ability he possessed. To know this truth is to dispel that myth that a Black man is incapable of leadership on an international scale.

In the beginning of the repopulation of the earth after the flood, it was a Black man who was successfully coordinating the most massive building project civilization had known. He was so successful in this endeavor (though it was against the expressed will of God) that God had to personally interrupt the venture. Look at what God said about the unity and cooperation that Nimrod had orchestrated.

"And the Lord said, Behold, the people is one, and they have all one language; and this they begin to do: and now nothing will be restrained from them, which they have imagined to do." Genesis 11:6

If the Christian publishers will be real caretakers of Biblical truth, they should picture Nimrod as a black-skinned man in their publications. Well, I know some will say it really doesn't matter whether he was Black or white and that it's the essence of the story that really matters. I agree that it is the essence of the story that matters and the color of Nimrod's skin is part of that essence.

Nimrod founded several cities, and it was the custom that the cities were populated by the descendants and relatives of its founder. One of the cities founded by Nimrod was the city of Nineveh, which we read about in the story of Jonah .

"Arise, go to Nineveh, that great city, and cry against it; for their wickedness is come up before me." Jonah 1:2

I thought at first reading this that it was an interesting footnote to the story of the Jonah situation. I do not think, however, that it is correct to imply that the reason Jonah did not want to go to Nineveh was because of the color of the people. However, it is most likely a correct assumption that the people of Nineveh were in fact people of color.

The Big Lie Told About Egypt

Millions of Americans have seen that famous motion picture titled "The Ten Commandments" with Charleton Heston portraying Moses and Yul Brenner portraying the Pharaoh. This could not be farther from the truth. After looking at that film, you would get the impression that the Egyptians were white and all the Jews were white.

Mizraim, a Black son of Ham, whose name is also translated Egypt, was the father of the Egyptian nation, a nation of people of color. Therefore, it is inconceivable that the Israelites were enslaved to a nation of whites. They were slaves to a nation of people of color, a nation of Black-skinned people.

With this being true, the great contributions of the Egyptians to civilization that have been discovered in the archaeological findings must be attributed to Black people. Even the paintings on the walls of the great pyramids clearly depict the characters as people of color.

Therefore, when I read in the Bible that a person was an Egyptian or looked like an Egyptian I know that it is talking about a person of dark skin. There are several famous men of God who were mistaken as being Egyptians, based on their appearance. Hold on to your hat as you read these next few paragraphs.

The Apostle Paul Mistaken as an Egyptian

"And as Paul was to be led into the castle, he said unto the chief captain, May I speak unto thee? Who said, Canst thou speak Greek?

Art not thou that Egyptian, which before these

days madest an uproar, and leddest out into the wilderness four thousand men that were murderers?" Acts 21:37-38

Moses Mistaken for an Egyptian

"And they said, An Egyptian delivered us out of the hand of the shepherds, and also drew water enough for us, and watered the flock." Exodus 2:19

Both the Apostle Paul and the Prophet Moses were mistaken on separate occasions for Egyptian men. This is alarming only to those who are not serious students of the Word of God and are not aware of the massive intermarrying that took place among the children of Israel and their Black neighbors.

It is highly probable that the nation of Israel was never a nation of lily-white people, but a race of people who were of color. This would explain the reason for certain statements and situations that occurred.

Think about this. Moses was born during the time when the Pharaoh had issued a decree to kill all the baby boys. Yet, the Pharaoh allowed his daughter to bring Moses into the palace to be brought up as a son. If Moses had been a white baby, wouldn't he have stood out like a sore thumb, and encountered the wrath of the Pharaoh?

Prejudiced Reference Books Give Illogical Reasons

I read the commentary in one reference Bible that said Moses was mistaken as an Egyptian because he was dressed in Egyptian clothing. This is the most ridiculous reason for this mistaken identity I have ever heard of, as if to say that if a white man dresses in African attire, that he would not be looked on as white but as a Black man.

It is superfluous to attempt to say that the Egyptian race was a race of exclusively white people because it is not a race of exclusively white people today. Look at pictures of the modern day Egyptian and you can clearly see distinct "Negroid" features. The Egyptians were a nation of creative, ingenious, black-skinned people who made a considerably significant contribution to civilization.

Famous Children of Mizraim (Egypt)

"And Mizraim begat Ludim, and Anamim, and Lehabim, and Naphtuhim,"

"And Pathrusim, and Casluhim, (out of whom came Philistim,) and Caphtorim." Genesis 10:13-14

"And Pathrusim, and Casluhim, (of whom came the Philistines,) and Caphthorim." I Chronicles 1:12

The Philistines

These passages reveal that the Philistines were direct descendants of Egypt (Mizraim), Ham's Black son. In most of the Christian literature the Philistines are pictured as a race of white people. I can hardly count the number of times I have seen a picture of David and Goliath, the giant Philistine warrior (I Samuel 17-19).

"Now Saul, and they, and all the men of Israel, were in the valley of Elah, fighting with the Philistines."

"And David rose up early in the morning, and left the sheep with a keeper, and took, and went, as Jesse had commanded him; and he came to the trench, as the host was going forth to the fight, and shouted for the battle."

"For Israel and the Philistines had put the battle in array, army against army."

"And David left his carriage in the hand of the keeper of the carriage, and ran into the army, and came and saluted his brethren."

"And as he talked with them, behold, there came up the champion, the Philistine of Gath, Goliath by name, out of the armies of the Philistines, and spake according to the same words: and David heard them." I Samuel 17:19-23

I have never once seen any portrayal of this giant warrior as the tall Black man that he was. Again, the American Euro-centric media and the movies paint a different picture of these clearly revealed truths from the Bible.

Another famous Philistine was a woman named Delilah, the woman who deceived Samson. To tell her story and to portray her as a white woman is to misrepresent the truth and distort the overall interpretation of the scripture.

When you eliminate these facts, you cause the little Black children who read these Bible stories to assume that Black people had no part in the history recorded in the Bible. This leaves them with the impression that they are not important and have little worth.

The Land of Canaan was a Black Civilization

Canaan was a son, a direct descendant, of Black Ham, which would make him a Black man. The land that was named for him would quite naturally be a land inhabited by his kindred which were black-skinned people. This is a very awesome awakening type of truth, that really testifies to the ability of Black people to build civilizations. While Israel was in slavery to the Egyptians (Black descendants of Mizraim) the Black Canaanites were constructing a massive civilization.

When the children of Israel left Egypt to possess the promised land, they were not going to a big ghetto or undeveloped civilization. They were going into a country that was highly developed agriculturally, architecturally, and socially. God described it to them as a land flowing with milk and honey where they would find houses that they did not build, cities that they did not construct, and gardens and vineyards that they did not plant.

Who planted these vineyards and built the cities and neighborhoods? It was the children (descendants) of the Black man Canaan. This should erase the old stereotype that blacks are destructive and can only create ghettos where-ever they go. Our Biblical heritage proves that Blacks are capable of much more.

Famous Children of Canaan

"And Canaan begat Sidon his firstborn, and Heth," Genesis 10:15

If you read through the fifteenth verse too quickly you will miss the mention of two of Canaan's children who fathered great nations of people. The reference books agree that **"Heth,"** one of Canaan's sons, was the father of the nation of the Hittites. Throughout the Israeli campaign of the promised land there are several mentionings of the Hittites, along with the Jebusites, the Amorites, the Girgasites, and others.

Uriah the Hittite

However, in II Samuel 11:3, there is the mention of a certain Hittite that makes an impression on Biblical history. His name is Uriah, the husband of Bathsheba, who was killed by King David to cover up his adultery. The story brings to light the faithfulness, the loyalty, and the integrity Uriah, a Black man, had for his country and his king.

Bathsheba, whose name carries within it part of the name of the son of Cush (Gen. 10:7), Sheba, highlights that this was a Black couple in whose life and marriage King David interfered. Remember the story shows that David attempted to deceive Uriah that his (David's child) who Bathsheba would give birth to, would be Uriah's. It would be highly unlikely that this deception would have been successful unless David was also a man of color.

How could a Black couple give birth to a white baby without arousing some suspicion? This would have been the case if David was as white as he is portrayed in books. I think that it is highly probable that David was indeed a man of color due in part to the aforementioned intermarrying issue. It would have been unlikely for this scheme to have worked successfully unless both men involved were of similar skin color.

Finally, after Uriah is murdered and buried, King David's sin is exposed and he repents before God. The baby conceived in the sin of David and Bathsheba dies and is buried. Bathsheba conceives again and has a child named Solomon who became the wisest man who ever lived. Think about this for a moment. If Solomon's mother was Black, that would make

Solomon the possessor of some Black genes too! This is amazing that the wisest man on record in Biblical history was a Black man, King Solomon.

The Black Canaanite Disciple

The next famous descendant of Canaan was the one disciple who traveled with Jesus during his earthly ministry. Read the mentioning of him in the following passage.

"Now the names of the twelve apostles are these; The first, Simon, who is called Peter, and Andrew his brother; James the son of Zebedee, and John his brother;"

"Phillip, and Bartholomew; Thomas and Matthew the publican; James the son of Alphaeus, and Lebbaeus, whose surname was Thaddaeus;"

"Simon the Canaanite, and Judas Iscariot, who also betrayed Him."

"These twelve Jesus sent forth, and commanded them, saying, Go not into the way of the Gentiles, and into any city of the Samaritans enter ye not:" Matthew 10:2-5

I think it is unfair that this Black disciple is not pictured anywhere in any Euro-centric depictions of the twelve disciples. It gives the impression that none of the twelve disciples were men of color and that the only man of color that had any notable interaction with Jesus was the Black man that carried the cross.

The Jebusites, the Builders of Jerusalem

"And the Jebusite, and the Amorite, and the Girgasite," Genesis 10:16

In verse sixteen, there are mentioned the Jebusites who were the descendants of Canaan, who also inhabited the land of Canaan. Many references agree that the children of Jebus were the original founders of the city of "Salem", later named Jerusalem. The origin of Jerusalem is referred to in the writings of the Prophet Ezekiel. He states that the mother of Jerusalem (Jebus), was a Hittite and the father of Jerusalem was an Amorite. As we have seen, both the Amorites and Hittites were Black nations.

"And say, Thus saith the Lord God unto Jerusalem; Thy birth and thy nativity is of the land of Canaan; thy father was an Amorite, and thy mother an Hittite." Ezekiel 16:3

Jerusalem was later captured and inhabited by the children of Israel. The account of the seizing of Jerusalem is found in the following passages.

"And the border went up by the valley of the son of Hinnom unto the south side of the Jebusite; the same is Jerusalem: and the border went up to the top of the mountain that lieth before the valley of Hinnom westward, which is at the end of the valley of the giants northward:" Joshua 15:8

"And Zelah, Eleph, and Jebusi, which is Jerusalem, Gibeath, and Kirjath; fourteen cities with their villages. This is the inheritance of the children of Benjamin according to their families." Joshua 18:28

"And the children of Benjamin did not drive out the Jebusites that inhabited Jerusalem; but the Jebusites dwell with the children of Benjamin in Jerusalem unto this day." Judges 1:21

It was the intermarrying of the Jebusites and the Benjamites that could have been the reason that the Apostle Paul, who was a Benjamite, was a dark skinned Jew. Note these two accounts:

"And the children of Israel dwelt among the Canaanites, Hittites, and Amorites, and

Perizzites, and Hivites, and Jebusites:"

"And they took their daughters to be their wives, and gave their daughters to their sons, and served their gods." Judges 3:5-6

The Black Canaanite Woman

Another passage in the Bible that we have read over without really understanding its significance is the account of Jesus with the Canaanite woman in the New Testament.

"Then Jesus went thence, and departed into the coasts of Tyre and Sidon.

And, behold, a woman of Canaan came out of the same coasts, and cried unto him, saying, Have mercy on me, O Lord, thou son of David; my daughter is grievously vexed with a devil." Matthew 15:21-22

The encounter with this woman of color shows the Master's concern about the needs of people. Its significance to a proper understanding of the ministry of Jesus and His availability to all people, including Black people, is of paramount importance.

As we continue on this trip through the Bible, it

is plain to see how the Holy Spirit is careful to make mention of the ancestral origin of certain people. We should be impressed with the importance of this kind of footnoting of truth. If the Spirit of God, who inspired the writing of the scripture, thought it important to make constant mention of the descendants of Ham, you and I should too!

Was the Black Race Cursed?

The most tragic lie that is being handed down to the Christian world is that the Black race of people is under an eternal curse. I have heard this from childhood and many people are very confused about this issue. The question is raised, "Are Black people suffering now because they were cursed?"

The reason for this confusion, is the gross misinterpretation of the incident between Noah and Ham. Here is the text:

"And Noah began to be an husbandman, and he planted a vineyard:

And he drank the wine, and was drunken; and he was uncovered within his tent.

And Ham, the father of Canaan, saw the

nakedness of his father, and told his two brethren without.

And Shem and Japheh took a garment, and laid it upon both their shoulders, and went backward, and covered the nakedness of their father; and their faces were backward, and they saw not their father's nakedness.

And Noah awoke from his wine, and knew what his younger son had done unto him.

And he said, Cursed be Canaan; a servant of servants shall he be unto his brethren.

And he said, Blessed be the Lord God of Shem; and Canaan shall be his servant." *Genesis 9:20-26*

The truth of what happened is that Ham, the father of the races of people of color, was never cursed. In fact, he was blessed by God along with his brothers. <u>What God has blessed no man can curse.</u> Simple study shows that it was Ham's son, Canaan, who was cursed and there is no indication that this curse was a perpetual curse upon generation after generation. The kind of sin that was committed by this son of Noah and the consequences are discussed under the terms of the old covenant law.

The major question is what did Ham do to warrant a curse upon his son? The answer to this question is found in the study of the phrase, "the nakedness of his father". Here are some supportive scriptures that will help us understand what actually happened.

"None of you shall approach to any that is near of kin to him, to uncover their nakedness: I am the Lord.

The nakedness of thy father, or the nakedness of thy mother, shalt thou not uncover: she is thy mother; thou shalt not uncover her nakedness.

The nakedness of thy father's wife shalt thou not uncover: it is thy father's nakedness." Leviticus 18:6-8

It appears that Ham looked upon Noah's naked wife, which was a forbidden thing then and was later incorporated into the law. Even though this occurred years before the law was issued, the moral order of God prohibited this act. The law also required that the punishment so described only applied to a specific generation. Based on scripture written on this subject by the same author, Moses, there is no reason to suppose that this curse extended past the generation it was levied upon.

Therefore, there is no reason to say that the entire Black race is suffering today because it is subject to an eternal curse. This lie must stop and the truth about what happened must be told. Many prejudiced white churches are using the misinterpretation of the incident as justification for anti-Black, anti-people of color sentiments. The thought that Black people are supposed to be servants and slaves is a cruel misrepresentation of scripture.

There are many examples of Canaanites and other Ham descendants experiencing God's spiritual and material blessings. Abraham was tremendously blessed by many of the Black descendants of Ham's sons.

Melchisedec King of SALEM

One of the most interesting figures in Biblical history is this man Melchisedec. His name is mentioned in highest regards in both the Old and New Testaments. In fact the New Testament compares Jesus to Melchisedec and declares Melchisedec to be greater than Abraham. Who is this person, greater than Abraham, who comes on the scene with prominence and importance?

"For this Melchisedec, king of Salem, priest of the most high God, who met Abraham returning

from the slaughter of the kings, and blessed him;"

"To whom also Abraham gave a tenth part of all; first being by interpretation King of righteousness, and after that also King of Salem, which is, King of peace;"

"Without father, without mother, without descent, having neither beginning of days, nor end of life; but made like unto the Son of God; abideth a priest continually."

"Now consider how great this man was, unto whom even the patriarch Abraham gave the tenth of the spoils."

"And verily they that are of the sons of Levi, who receive the office of the priesthood, have a commandment to take tithes of the people according to the law, that is, of their brethren, though they come out of the loins of Abraham:"

"But he whose descent is not counted from them received tithes of Abraham, and blessed him that had the promises."

"And without all contradiction the less is blessed of the better." Hebrews 7:1-7

The scripture bears record that this man was of supreme importance in the plan of God. I was shocked to learn that he was not a "spiritual being" that appeared out of the spirit world as some have taught. He was a real man who was both a King and a Priest of a place called Salem.

It is a widely accepted fact that Salem refers to a place that would be later renamed Jerusalem. Jerusalem and Salem both reference that same place.

"In Salem also is His tabernacle, and His dwelling place in Zion." Psalm 76:2

At the historical time of this encounter between Abraham and Melchizedek in the land of Canaan, Salem, as well as all of the Canaanite cities, was ruled and inhabited by Black men. This would make Melchizedek a man of color who both ruled his city, Salem, and functioned in the office of a Priest before Almighty God.

The impact of this truth is astounding when you understand the significant role that this Black man makes upon Biblical history. The story revealed that Abraham had received the promise from God but did not fully understand all that God would do through him. Abraham had won a great victory over several kings and had rescued his nephew Lot in Genesis 14:16. He was returning with the spoils of the battle when God arranged an appointment with His Priest to share insight and revelation with Abraham.

"And the king of Sodom went out to meet him after his return from the slaughter of Chedorlaomer, and of the kings that were with him, at the valley of Shaveh, which is the king's dale."

And Melchizedek king of Salem brought forth bread and wine: and he was the priest of the most high God."

"And he blessed him, and said, Blessed be Abram of the most high God, possessor of heaven and earth:"

"And blessed be the most high God, which hath delivered thine enemies into thy hand. And he gave him tithes of all." Genesis 14:17-20

This meeting shows the superior spiritual wisdom and insight that this Black King had in the things of God. He ministers to Abraham, the first type of the Lord's Supper, and blesses Abraham and receives from Abraham the tithes, hundreds of years before the tithes were incorporated into the law. Further, when Jesus discussed Abraham with the Pharisees and scribes he said to them that he was greater than Abraham and told them that Abraham had seen his day.

"Art thou greater than our father Abraham, which is dead? and the prophets are dead: whom makest thou thyself? John 8:53

Your father Abraham rejoiced to see my day: and he saw it, and was glad.

Then said the Jews unto him, Thou art not yet fifty years old, and hast thou seen Abraham?

Jesus said unto them, Verily, verily, I say unto you, Before Abraham was, I am." John 8:56-58

The Pharisees did not understand how Jesus could make such a statement because he was so young, and Abraham was already dead and buried. What I believe Jesus was speaking of was the day that Abraham visited with Melchizedek and was ministered to about the gospel of Jesus. This would explain how Abraham was saved by faith. The Bible records that faith comes by hearing the Word of God. Somebody had to tell Abraham about God's plan, he had to accept it, and thus he became the father (the example) of those saved by faith.

God used this Black man, Melchizedek, King of Salem and Priest of the Most High God, to introduce the revelation of Jesus to Abraham. Again this shows that men of color had a relationship with God and were used of God long before the missionaries <u>invaded Africa and long before Blacks came to America.</u>

King Abimelech and Abraham

"And Abraham journeyed from thence toward the south country, and dwelled between Kadesh and Shur, and sojourned in Gerar."

"And Abraham said of Sarah his wife, She is my sister: and Abimelech king of Gerar sent, and took Sarah."

"But God came to Abimelech in a dream by night, and said to him, Behold, thou art but a dead man, for the woman which thou hast taken; for she is a man's wife."

"But Abimelech had not come near her: and he said, Lord, wilt thou slay also a righteous nation?"

Said he not unto me, She is my sister? and she, even she herself said, He is my brother: in the integrity of my heart and innocency of my hands have I done this."

"And God said unto him in a dream, Yea, I know that thou didst this in the integrity of thy heart; for I also withheld thee from sinning against me: therefore suffered I thee not to touch her."

"Now therefore restore the man his wife; for he is a prophet, and he shall pray for thee, and thou shalt live: and if thou restore her not, know thou that thou shalt surely die, thou, and all that are thine."

"Therefore Abimelech rose early in the morning, and called all his servants, and told all these things in their ears: and the men were sore afraid." Genesis 20:1-8

Many Bible students will remember the confrontation that Abraham had with this King of Gerar. Gerar was a Philistine city inhabited by Philistines who were descendants of the Black man Ham. King Abimelech was the Black ruler of this Black city into which Abraham sojourned. There are several interesting things about this encounter with this Black King who possessed impeccable character that is most impressive.

The story goes that Abraham conspired with Sarah to lie about their relationship. For fear of his life, Abraham and Sarah agreed to say that they were brother and sister instead of husband and wife. This was a half-truth because the Bible does record that they were half brother and sister, having the same father.

"And yet indeed she is my sister; she is the daughter of my father, but not the daughter of my mother; and she became my wife." Genesis 20:12

The fact that God revealed the truth to this Black King implies that this King had a relationship with God, which proves that there were Godly Black people in the Old Testament. The fifth and sixth verses show that this King had integrity and innocence before God to such a degree that God would not allow Abraham's deception to cause this man to stumble.

Another interesting point in this narrative is that Abimelech obviously was a man who possessed a giving heart. The fourteenth and fifteenth verses show a demonstration of this man's overflowing generosity as he gives abundantly to Abraham.

Ephron the Hittite

The Hittite that sold Abraham the burial ground

was a man called Ephron (Gen 23:7-15). When Sarah (the wife of Abraham) died in Hebron in the land of Canaan, Abraham, a stranger in the land, requested of the children of Heth (Hittites), a place to bury his wife. The children of Heth were the descendants of the Black man Ham's son, Canaan (Gen 10:15).

There was no doubt a relationship existed between Abraham and these Black Canaanites, in that Ephron the Hittite, (name given to the descendants of Heth), wanted to give the burial ground to Abraham at no charge. Again, this is another witness to the giving nature of these people of color in Abraham's day.

CHAPTER V

Was Jesus White or Black?

CHAPTER V
Was Jesus White Or Black?

If you knew of a lie that was being told that was prohibiting a person from giving his life to Jesus, would you do all you could to tell that person the truth? This is a question that we have posed several times during this book. This chapter is probably the most important chapter relative to this question.

Thus far we have established that man was created in the beginning as a man of color. Even the scientists have agreed that a Black woman was the mother of all living. It does not appear that there were any color prejudices that existed in the Bible. It is quite difficult for blacks in America to imagine a society where there is no color prejudice.

It is an awesome thing to see how the Holy Spirit leaves a trail of information to track these descendants of Ham throughout the Bible. I believe God knew that the color of skin would be used to divide people. Careful study of the Word of God shows clearly that color of skin does not determine worth. The Bible shows that God uses men and women of color to carry out his plan. This illustrates that color is not a factor. Knowledge of this is critical to overcome the prejudicial influences of a society that makes color an issue. Further, for those who have been victims of the mental oppression, that color of skin renders you either acceptable or unacceptable, this truth is essential to self-appreciation and personal dignity.

Oppression always takes place by consent. This consent may be passive, but it is consent none-the-less! The "Euro-Systemic Influences" have bombarded the thinking of people of color with misinformation that has convinced many that the color of one's skin is a factor with God. Many Blacks have failed to attempt success because they feel that even in the plan of God they are at best, an afterthought.

Most Blacks think that the Bible is a book about all white people and that there is very little in the Bible that pertains to Black people. Therefore, the average Black Christian has been lulled into a sense of second-class worth and a passive acceptance of oppression from this society.

The Mental Chains of Slavery

Slavery is not solely enforced with physical chains, but also with mental chains. Until a slave accepts his captivity, the physical chains must be kept in place to prevent his escape because the slave is still thinking freedom. It is only when he mentally accepts his captivity that the chains can be removed, the gate left open, and the slave master can rest assured that the slave will not escape. You can remove the physical barriers resulting from slavery in America, but until the mental barriers are removed, the experience of freedom cannot be enjoyed.

The power to define and set the rules is the power to determine the destiny of all those who must live by those rules.

In this society, the standards for acceptability are defined by the white majority, and it has been extremely difficult and next to impossible for many Blacks to measure up to this unfair standard. For instance, if the standard of beauty is light color skin, straight texture of hair, and thin lips, it is impossible for many Blacks to measure up to this standard.

As a Black man, I was born naturally without those physical features. If then I want to have a good self-image and a sense of being accepted, I must reject this white society's standard of worth and accept God's standard as shown in His Word.

When this is done, there will be room for development and the release of potentials that would otherwise remained harnessed. I have watched many Black ministers court with a passion the white Christian media to gain acceptability and credibility. There is the unspoken thought that, "my ministry has not really arrived until Oral Roberts, Pat Robertson, or some other renowned white minister sanctions what I am doing." To gain the self-worth that pleases God, this kind of thinking and pursuit of worth must be abandoned.

This sounds easy, but it is not as easy as it sounds in that my thinking has been so influenced by this oppressive society that it requires a major effort to think independently of the standards of this society. It is more comfortable to attempt to alter my looks, my speech, my worship and my attitude to conform to the standard that is widely accepted, than to experience the trauma of rejecting the standards.

To think independently is viewed by this society as rebellion against God.

In most homes in America and in most churches in America and in many countries that are influenced by the Euro-centric culture, there are pictures of a "white-skinned" Jesus. This representation is widely accepted as the real picture of the Son of God. Many have innocently accepted this as the picture of the Son of God without understanding that not only is this incorrect, but it is also unscriptural.

Thousands upon thousands of Black males are flocking to the Islamic religion because they believe that the Christian faith is a white man's gospel. It is very rare, even in the traditional Black church settings, that anyone will ever talk about Black people in the Bible. So with the misinformation that the Bible is a white man's book, about all-white people, with a white Jesus and His twelve all-white disciples, it is no wonder that Blacks in this radical generation would reject, on the surface, Christianity.

Now, those of us who are spiritual understand that God is not concerned with color and that Jesus is not to be accepted based on what color he was may find it difficult to see the relevance in this point. We must not ignore Satan's desire to do everything he can to prevent mankind from accepting Jesus as Lord. A Black man who has had some bad experiences with the white race may see a white man, a white Jesus, as the object of his oppression. It is most difficult, (next to impossible) to relate to Christ spiritually when you are not born again.

This is not to say that every Black man who rejects Jesus does it on the basis of the white man's portrayal. One Black person being hindered by this depiction is too many, especially when to picture Jesus in this way, or any way, is against the expressed will of God. Once we are exposed to truth, we are accountable to operate in that truth, no matter how long we have operated in error.

Was the Selection of the Body of Jesus Imporant?

Was the selection of the body of Jesus very important in the plan of God? I think that everything associated with the life of Jesus was of critical importance. If a Black person is subhuman and inferior, then for Jesus to be born in such a body would hinder God's plan to save mankind. Further, it was with great care that God selected the family and the ancestors of Jesus. You must remember that Jesus was planned from the foundation of the world, so this was no incidental matter.

When careful examination is made of the ancestors of Jesus, it is amazing that there are several "Black people" in his family tree. These descendants of Ham in the genealogy of Jesus prove that by this society's standard, Jesus was a man of color. The picture that is marketed of Jesus is definitely in error because it is just the portrait of an Italian model that was never selected on the basis of any Biblical or historical data. Likewise, it is highly improbable that the Last Supper took place as it is depicted in the popular artist rendition.

To properly study the genealogy of Jesus, it must be done by addressing the lineage through Mary and not Joseph. Joseph was the adopted father of Jesus and actually had no physical or genetic participation in the body of Jesus. If you look at the genealogy recorded in Matthew the first chapter, it is the linage of Joseph. The family tree recorded in Luke, chapter one, at first glance looks like the genealogy of Joseph, but there is a key statement that proves otherwise.

"The book of the generation of Jesus Christ, the son of David, the son of Abraham.

And Jacob begat Joseph the husband of Mary, of whom was born Jesus, who is called Christ."
Matthew 1:1,16

Luke's Account:
"And Jesus himself began to be about thirty years of age, being (as was supposed) the son of

Joseph, <u>which was the son of Heli.</u>" Luke 3:23

Heli was the father of Mary, because Matthew records that Jacob was the natural father who begat Joseph. The scripture never says that Heli begat Joseph. Other reference sources agree that Heli was the father-in-law of Joseph. This then would make the genealogy recorded here reflect Mary's background and not her husband.

"Which was the son of Jesse, which was the son of Obed, which was the son of Booz, which was the son of Salmon, which was the son of Naasson," Luke 3:32

Note that in Luke 3, verse 32, there is the mention of a man named Salmon whose son was Booz. Booz had to be a man of color because of his mother, a Canaanite woman, named Rahab (Rachab). Rahab was the Black Canaanite woman who assisted the children of Israel in taking Jericho. Rahab and her family were saved and accepted among the children of Israel after the overthrow of Jericho.

"But Joshua had said unto the two men that had spied out the country, Go into the harlot's house, and bring out thence the woman, and all that she hath, as ye sware unto her.

And the young men that were spies went in, and brought out Rahab, and her father, and her mother, and her brethren, and all that she had; and they brought out all her kindred, and left them without the camp of Israel.

And they burnt the city with fire, and all that was therein: only the silver, and the gold, and the vessels of brass and of iron, they put into the treasury of the house of the Lord.

And Joshua saved Rahab the harlot alive, and her father's household, and all that she had; and she dwelleth in Israel even unto this day; because she hid the messengers, which Joshua sent to spy out Jericho." Joshua 6:22-25

It is also likely that David and Solomon, who were in the lineage of Jesus, were men of color as we have mentioned in another chapter. Because of the intermarrying and the known Black genes flowing in the lineage of Jesus, it is likely that Jesus was a man of color. In other countries, Jesus and Mary are both depicted as being of color. Think about this passage:

"And when they were departed, behold, the angel of the Lord appeareth to Joseph in a dream, saying, Arise, and take the young child and his mother, and flee into Egypt, and be

thou there until I bring thee word: for Herod will seek the young child to destroy him.

When he arose, he took the young child and his mother by night, and departed into Egypt:

And was there until the death of Herod: that it might be fulfilled which was spoken of the Lord by the prophet, saying, Out of Egypt have I called my son. " Matthew 2:13-15

When there was an all-out search for the Jesus child by Herod, the angel of the Lord told Joseph to take Jesus and hide in the land of Egypt. Think about it. Why would you attempt to hide a little white baby in a land inhabited by mostly Black people? You are probably smarter than that, and you know God is smarter than you are. The pertinent truth of this chapter is not whether Jesus was Black or white, but it is unscriptural to draw portraits of him.

Why You Should not Paint A Picture of Jesus

Most Christians are not at all aware that it is against the expressed will of God to paint pictures of Jesus or make an image of Him. The deity of Jesus is equated to that of God. Jesus spoke often of his oneness with the Father:

"I and my Father are one." John 10:30

"And the glory which thou gavest me I have given them; that they may be one, even as we are one:" John 17:22

Thou shalt not make unto thee any graven image, or any image, or any likeness of any thing that is in heaven above, or that is in the earth beneath, or that is in the water under the earth:" Exodus 20:4

God gave the specific mandate that deity should not be expressed or made into or in the likeness of a graven image. Jesus would be considered as much deity as God the Father himself and therefore, should not be so pictured.

Further, the Holy Spirit makes this point absolutely clear under the new testament in Acts 17:29-30.

"Forasmuch then as we are the offspring of God, we ought not to think that the Godhead is like unto gold, or silver, or stone, graven by art and man's device.

And the times of this ignorance God winked at; but now commandeth all men every where to repent: " Acts 17:29-30

These scriptures make the point with crystal clarity that it is improper to paint a picture of Jesus, Black or white. Therefore, all the pictures of Jesus that are hanging in homes of millions of Americans and in thousands of Churches should be removed. These may be stumbling blocks in the acceptance of Jesus into a person's life.

There are good reasons why not painting pictures of Jesus is the best policy. Since salvation is solely dependent on the acceptance of Jesus as savior and Lord, all interferences should be removed. If there are no pictures painted, there will be no misrepresentation, and thus no stumbling blocks.

To paint Jesus as a white man could be an offense to the Black people. To paint Him as a Black man could be an offense to white people. Therefore, the best policy is to obey the Word of God and leave off painting portraits or making graven images of Jesus.

Man is totally incapable of portraying the essence of Jesus on an artist's canvas. The essence of who Jesus is supersedes that which can be placed on the canvas. Jesus said that he was the Bread of Life, the Living Water, the Way, and the Truth. Now how can you capture that on a canvas?

So, if you have a picture of a white Jesus or a Black Jesus, it should be removed and destroyed immediately.

We have established that because of the widespread intermarrying among the people of the Bible, there were probably many color shades of people. Many outstanding men of God who were Jews are recorded as marrying Black Hamitic women, which would cause their children to have "Black genes" (genes from their Black parent).

Abraham Had Two Black Wives

Most avid Bible readers know of the initial challenges that Abraham and Sarah had with producing the promised son. During a period of frustration, Sarah convinced Abraham to take her handmaiden to be his wife so that she could bear him a son. So, Abraham married Hagar, an Egyptian woman, who became part of Biblical history by giving birth to Ishmael, who was also blessed of God. The actual story is recorded in Gen.16:1.

It should be noted that Ishmael, the son of Abraham and Hagar, the Egyptian, had to be a man of color.

There is another Black woman in Abraham's life that is little spoken of named Keturah. Keturah gave birth to many children who also became many great and powerful Black nations.

Keturah's Children

"Then again Abraham took a wife, and her name was Keturah."

And she bare him Zimran, and Jokshan, and Medan, and Midian, and Ishbak, and Shuah.

And Jokshan begat Sheba, and Dedan. And the sons of Dedan were Asshurim, and Letushim, and Leummim.

And the sons of Midian; Ephah, and Epher and Hanroch, and Abidah and Eldaash. All these were the children of Keturah. Genesis 25:1-3

I don't think it is presumptuous to say that these were Black nations because in our culture, when a Black woman gives birth to a child by a white man the child is considered a Black child.

Moses Married a Black Woman

Moses married a Black woman whose name was Zipporah, and she was a descendant of one of

Keturah's sons, Midian. When Moses left Egypt after being exposed for killing the Egyptian soldier, he went to the land of the Midianites. There he married one of the daughters of the Priest of Midian, Jethro, whose name is also translated Reuel.

"Now when Pharaoh heard this thing, he sought to slay Moses. But Moses fled from the face of Pharaoh, and dwelt in the land of Midian: and he sat down by a well.

Now the priest of Midian had seven daughters: and they came and drew water, and filled the troughs to water their father's flock.

And the shepherds came and drove them away: but Moses stood up and helped them, and watered their flock.

And when they came to Reuel their father, he said, How is it that ye are come so soon to day?

And they said, An Egyptian delivered us out of the hand of the shepherds, and also drew water enough for us, and watered the flock.

And he said unto his daughters, And where is he? why is it that ye have left the man? call him, that he may eat bread.

And Moses was content to dwell with the man: and he gave Moses Zipporah his daughter.

And she bare him a son, and he called his name Gershom: for he said, I have been a stranger in a strange land." Exodus 2:15-22

"When Jethro, the priest of Midian, Moses' father in law, heard of all that God had done for Moses, and for Israel his people, and that the Lord had brought Israel out of Egypt;

Then Jethro, Moses' father in law, took Zipporah, Moses' wife, after he had sent her back,

And her two sons; of which the name of the one was Gershom; for he said, I have been an alien in a strange land:

And the name of the other was Eliezer; for the God of my father, said he, was mine help, and delivered me from the sword of Pharaoh:" Exodus 18:1-4

"And Miriam and Aaron spake against Moses because of the Ethiopian woman whom he had married: for he had married an Ethiopian woman." Numbers 12:1

Aaron and Miriam got into serious trouble with God because they talked against Moses' Ethiopian wife. The disagreement was probably not about the color of her skin, but about her nationality. This does not, however, exclude the fact that Ethiopians were Black people who were descendants of Cush, the son of Ham.

Moses had two Black sons by this woman. Their names were <u>Gershom</u> and <u>Eliezer</u>. This would make the Jews born from these two sons a dark-skinned race of people, providing further reason why there were many dark-skinned Jews.

Remember the issue here is not nationality, since it appears that in some Biblical cases the children took on the nationality of their father.

The issue here is their probable color of skin which was, no doubt, "one of color" since they descended from a people of color.

Esau Marries Three Black Women

I found it most interesting that Esau's marriages offended his mother Rebekah. This is what influenced her to assist Jacob in deceiving his father Isaac into giving him the birthright blessing. The issue with Rebekah was not one of color, but it was that Esau married outside their nationality.

"And Esau was forty years old when he took to wife Judith the daughter of Beeri the Hittite, and Bashemath the daughter of Elon the Hittite:

Which were a grief of mind unto Isaac and to Rebekah. " Genesis 26:34-35

"Now these are the generations of Esau, who is Edom.

Esau took his wives of the daughters of Canaan; Adah the daughter of Elon the Hittite, and Aholibamah the daughter of Anah the daughter of Zibeon the Hivite;

And Bashemath Ishmael's daughter, sister of Nebajoth.

And Adah bare to Esau Eliphaz; and Bashemath bare Reuel;

And Aholibamah bare Jeush, and Jaalam, and Korah: these are the sons of Esau, which were born unto him in the land of Canaan.

And Esau took his wives, and his sons, and his daughters, and all the persons of his house, and his cattle, and all his beasts, and all his substance, which he had got in the land of Canaan; and went into the country from the face of his brother Jacob.

For their riches were more than that they might dwell together; and the land wherein they were strangers could not bear them because of their cattle.

Thus dwelt Esau in mount Seir: Esau is Edom.

And these are the generations of Esau the father of the Edomites in mount Seir:" Genesis 36:1-9

Esau's descendants became known as the Edomites whom we see appear later in the history of the children of Israel as their enemies. Again it is not far-fetched to say that these were people of color.

The more we unfold this story of intermarrying, the more we see the Bible being a book of people of color and not a book exclusively about white people. We have already pointed out that David married the Black woman Bathsheba, and later gave birth to Solomon. A casual study of King Solomon's life shows his massive intermarrying with Black women.

"But king Solomon loved many strange women,

together with the daughter of Pharaoh, women of the Moabites, Ammonites, Edomites, Zidonians, and Hittites;

Of the nations concerning which the Lord said unto the children of Israel, Ye shall not go into them, neither shall they come in unto you: for surely they will turn away your heart after their gods: Solomon clave unto these in love.

And he had seven hundred wives, princesses, and three hundred concubines: and his wives turned away his heart." I Kings 11:1-3

Should Races of People Intermarry?

Although Israel was warned not to intermarry with those outside of their nation, they did so time and time again. Some prejudiced theologians use this warning that God gave Israel to support the prohibition of intermarrying among the races today. It appears that God's warning was not so that any race would be preserved "pure", because with God there is no respecter of persons and there is but one race of people. The aforementioned warning was given to help Israel to guard their commitment to God, so they would not be tempted to serve the idol gods of their marital partners.

To use the scriptures to prohibit intermarrying would also mean the people should not enter into contracts with other people outside of their race.

"Observe thou that which I command thee this day: behold, I drive out before thee the Amorite, and the Canaanite, and the Hittite, and the Perizzite, and the Hivite, and the Jebusite.

Take heed to thyself, lest thou make a covenant with the inhabitants of the land whither thou goest, lest it be for a snare in the midst of thee:

But ye shall destroy their altars, break their images, and cut down their groves:

For thou shalt worship no other god: for the Lord, whose name is Jealous, is a jealous God:

Lest thou make a covenant with the inhabitants of the land, and they go a whoring after their gods, and do sacrifice unto their gods, and one call thee, and thou eat of his sacrifice;

And thou take of their daughters unto thy sons, and their daughters go a whoring after their gods, and make thy sons go a whoring after their gods." Exodus 34:11-16

If you use part of this verse to support a narrow

view of marriage, then you must also use it to govern business activities also. You and I both know that this was not the spirit of the mandate of what God was establishing for all generations.

Two Black Tribes of Israel Through Joseph

The story of Jacob and his twelve sons, whose name is later changed to Israel, is quite interesting and spans many pages of the Old Testament. It is most interesting how some people of color (black-skinned) became a part of the children of promise through one of Jacob's sons. Jacob's son, Joseph, was sold into slavery by his brothers. Later, after suffering many things over a period of years, God elevated Joseph to be the Prime Minister of the land of Egypt.

The family was united in Egypt after several years when the brothers were sent to Egypt to buy food during the great famine. It was during this time that Joseph recognized his brothers, forgave them and invited them to come to Egypt to live with him. They accepted his offer and were given the land of Goshen by the Pharaoh.

When Jacob (Israel) had grown very old and was near death, he adopted the sons of Joseph who were born to him of his **Egyptian wife, Asenath.**

Ephraim and Manasseh were the two Black sons of Joseph.

"And Pharaoh called Joseph's name Zaphnath-paaneah; and he gave him to wife Asenath the daughter of Poti-pherah priest of On. And Joseph went out over all the land of Egypt." Genesis 41:45

"And unto Joseph were born two sons before the years of famine came, which Asenath the daughter of Poti-pherah priest of On bare unto him.

And Joseph called the name of the firstborn Manasseh: For God, said he, hath made me forget all my toil, and all my father's house.

And the name of the second called he Ephraim: For God hath caused me to be fruitful in the land of my affliction. " Genesis 41:50-52

And unto Joseph in the land of Egypt were born Manasseh and Ephraim, which Asenath the daughter of Poti-pherah priest of On bare unto him. " Genesis 46:20

These two sons of Joseph, Ephraim and Manesseh, received their portion in the promised land along with the rest of the children of Israel.

Remember now that these were children of a Black woman and therefore, they must have been Black. So then, the tribes of Ephraim and Manasseh were fathered by these two Black sons of Joseph, and were numbered with the tribes of Israel.

"Of the children of Joseph, namely, of the children of Ephraim, by their generations, after their families, by the house of their fathers, according to the number of the names, from twenty years old and upward, all that were able to go forth to war;

Those that were numbered of them, even of the tribe of Ephraim, were forty thousand and five hundred.

Of the children of Manasseh, by their generations, after their families, by the house of their fathers, according to the number of the names, from twenty years old and upward, all that were able to go forth to war;

Those that were numbered of them, even of the tribe of Manasseh, were thirty and two thousand and two hundred." Numbers 1:32-35

There were many famous Biblical heroes who came from the tribe of Ephraim. One well-known man was Joshua, the son of Nun. Joshua is known for his time of ministry to Moses and for eventually leading the entire nation to the promised land. This is an awesome fact that a man of color would be leading the children into the promised land and actually supervising the disbursing of the land of promise among the tribes of Israel.

Remember we are discussing the color factor in this writing to prove that the color of skin is not a factor of character. Therefore, in that God chose to use this man who is from a tribe that is fathered by a Black man, it should be clear that Black-skinned people are not inferior. The significant role that Joshua plays in his generation is an example of the major contribution that people of color have made in the plan of God.

Caleb - Joshua's Friend, a Man of Color

Although I have read the story of the Kadesh-Barnea scene where the children of Israel chose to believe the evil report of unbelieving spies, I never knew Caleb was a man of color. It is assumed that because Caleb represented one of the tribes of Israel as a spy, that Caleb was an Israelite.

Careful study reveals that Caleb was the son of Jephunneh, the Kenezite.

"Then the children of Judah came unto Joshua in Gilgal: and <u>Caleb the son of Jephunneh the Kenezite</u> said unto him, Thou knowest the thing that the Lord said unto Moses the man of God concerning me and thee in Kadesh-barnea." Joshua 14:6

"Save Caleb the son of Jephunneh the Kenezite, and Joshua the son of Nun: for they have wholly followed the Lord." Numbers 32:12

The Kenezites were distant descendants of the Edomites, a group of people of color who were inhabitants of the promised land.

"In the same day the Lord made a covenant with Abram, saying, Unto thy seed have I given this land, from the river of Egypt unto the great river, the river Euphrates:

The Kenites, and the Kenizzites, and the Kadmonites,

And the Hittites, and the Perizzites, and the Rephaims,

And the Amorites, and the Canaanites, and the

Girgashites, and the Jebusites." Genesis 15:18-21

It was this Black man, Caleb, who, along with Joshua, returned from spying out the land with a good report. These two men made their mark on Biblical history, but it is not known by most Christians that both men were Black.

CHAPTER VI

God's Strategic Use of the Black Man

CHAPTER VI
God's Strategic Use Of the Black Man

It is a truth that God is no respecter of persons as it relates to his promises, his provisions and his principles. However, no one will argue the fact that God reserves the right to select certain people, nations, or persons to do specific tasks. Everybody who is a part of the Christian faith understands that God made the choice of Abraham to do something special through him to bless the world.

"Now the Lord had said unto Abram, Get thee out of thy country, and from thy kindred, and from thy father's house, unto a land that I will shew thee:

And I will make of thee a great nation, and I will bless thee, and make thy name great; and thou shalt be a blessing:" **Genesis 12:1-2**

Further, it is recorded over and over again that God has made a choice of the nation of Israel for His divine purpose.

"For thou art an holy people unto the Lord thy God, and the Lord hath chosen thee to be a

peculiar people unto himself, above all the nations that are upon the earth." Deuteronomy 14:2

Let's begin a search through the scriptures to discover some strategic uses of men and women of color in the plan of God. You will plainly see that there is a common thread that links these situations together. This commonality supports the **"declared"** divine purpose for which God has chosen to use many Black men in his plan for mankind's redemption. I submit to you that just as God had made choice of Abraham and his seed for a specific purpose, so does it appear that God chose to use people of color to function in a particular role in His redemption plan.

Rules for Interpretation

Proper and orderly interpretation of scripture must follow certain guidelines. A statement of Biblical truth must be confirmed by both **"precept"** and **"example."** The precept is the clearly stated truth in the scripture. The example is the illustration of that stated truth. For example, the scripture states that the believer shall pray for the sick. This is the precept (Mark 16:18). The various instances of all the disciples and the apostles praying and ministering to the sick are the examples. Thus the Biblical truth is confirmed that the believers are to lay hands on and pray for the sick and they shall recover.

God Uses Melchizedek to Minister to Abraham

"And he brought back all the goods, and also brought again his brother Lot, and his goods, and the women also, and the people.

And the king of Sodom went out to meet him after his return from the slaughter of Chedorlaomer, and of the kings that were with him, at the valley of Shaveh, which is the king's dale.

And Melchizedek king of Salem brought forth bread and wine: and he was the priest of the most high God.

And he blessed him, and said, Blessed be Abram of the most high God, possessor of heaven and earth:

And blessed be the most high God, which hath delivered thine enemies into thy hand. And he gave him tithes of all. " Genesis 14:16-20

The scripture bears record that this man was of supreme importance in the plan of God. It was shocking to me to know that he was not a "spiritual being" that appeared out of the spirit world as some have taught. He was a real man who was both a King and a Priest of a place called Salem.

It is a widely accepted fact that Salem refers to the place that would be later renamed Jerusalem. Jerusalem and Salem both reference that same place. (Psalm 76:2)

"In Salem also His tabernacle, and His dwelling pace in Zion." Psalm 76:2

At the historical time of this encounter between Abraham and Melchizedec in the land of Canaan, Salem as well as the Canaanite cities were ruled and inhabited by Black men. This would make Melchizedec a man of color who both ruled his city, Salem, and functioned in the office of Priest before Almighty God.

The impact of this truth is astounding when you understand the significant role that this Black man makes upon Biblical history. The story reveals that Abraham had received the promise from God but did not fully understand all that God would do through him. Abraham had won a great victory over several kings and had rescued his nephew Lot and in Genesis 14:16, he was returning with the spoils of the battle when

God arranged an appointment with His Priest to share insight and revelation with Abraham.

This meeting shows the superior spiritual wisdom and insight that this Black king had in the things of God. He ministers to Abraham the first type of the Lord's Supper, and blesses Abraham and receives from Abraham the tithes hundreds of years before the tithes were incorporated into the law.

God used this Black man, Melchizedek, King of Salem and Priest of the Most High God, to introduce the revelation of Jesus to Abraham.

Why is the King of Salem Black?

In chapter four we traced the origin of Jerusalem back to the time it was called Salem, inhabited by Black people. Ezekiel refers to their heritage as the mother of Jerusalem being a Hittite and the father being an Amorite.

"And say, Thus saith the Lord God unto Jerusalem; Thy birth and thy nativity is of the land of Canaan; thy father was an Amorite, and thy mother an Hittite." Ezekiel 16:3

God chose Abraham to be His example for His generation and to bring to pass the promise of

God in the earth. Abraham had just confronted several armies who had taken Lot hostage and was victorious in his rescue efforts. He had labored with the frustration of not fully understanding the promise of God to him or having the faith that was required to receive that promise. As he was returning from the battle laden with the spoils of his victory, he recognized the King of Salem, the Priest of the Most High God to whom he owed the tithe of his increase.

He stopped and was ministered to by the King of Salem in such a powerful way that it changed the course of his life. He understands now who this promised seed would be and knew that his faith was required to receive what God had promised.

Melchizedek, a Black Man, Serves the First Communion in Scripture

God used this Black man to minister to Abraham and set him on his course of destiny and through this encounter Abraham became the father of the faithful.

Abimelech blesses Abraham

"And Abraham journeyed from thence toward the south country, and dwelled between Kadesh and

Shur, and sojourned in Gerar.

And Abraham said of Sarah his wife, She is my sister: and Abimelech king of Gerar sent, and took Sarah.

But God came to Abimelech in a dream by night, and said to him, Behold, thou art but a dead man, for the woman which thou has taken; for she is a man's wife.

But Abimelech had not come near her: and he said, Lord, wilt thou slay also a righteous nation?

Said he not unto me, She is my sister? and she, even she herself said, He is my brother: in the integrity of my heart and innocency of my hands have I done this.

And God said unto him in a dream, Yea, I know that thou didst this in the integrity of thy heart; for I also withheld thee from sinning against me: therefore suffered I thee not to touch her.

Now therefore restore the man his wife; for he is a prophet, and he shall pray for thee, and thou shalt live; and if thou restore her not, know thou that thou shalt surely die, thou, and all that are thine.

Therefore Abimelech rose early in the morning, and called all his servants, and told all these things in their ears: and the men were sore afraid.

Then Abimelech called Abraham, and said unto him, What has thou done unto us? and what have I offended thee, that thou has brought on me and on my kingdom a great sin? thou hast done deeds unto me that ought not to be done.

And Abimelech said unto Abraham, What sawest thou, that thou hast done this thing?

And Abraham said, Because I thought, Surely the fear of God is not in this place; and they will slay me for my wife's sake.

And yet indeed she is my sister; she is the daughter of my father, but not the daughter of my mother; and she became my wife.

And it came to pass, when God caused me to wander from my father's house, that I said unto her, This is thy kindness which thou shalt shew unto me; at every place whither we shall come, say of me, He is my brother.

And Abimelech took sheep, and oxen, and menservants and womenservants, and gave them unto Abraham, and restored him Sarah his wife.

And Abimelech said, Behold, my land is before thee: dwell where it pleaseth thee." Genesis 20:1-15

This next scene found Abraham in a very compromising position as he stretched the truth to avoid what he believed was a life-threatening situation. Abraham was in the land of Canaan and in the presence of this Black King Abimelech. Abimelech was the king of Gera, a city established by the Philistines who were descendants of Ham. Abimelech takes Abraham's wife as his concubine because Abraham lied and told him Sarah was his sister. (This was stretching the truth because in reality she was his half-sister)

Later, when the King thought to bring Sarah unto himself, the Lord appeared to him and told him that he was about to defile that which was special to God. Abimelech repented on the basis of his ignorance and the integrity of his heart. I like that because here is a Black man that could talk to God about his past record of integrity. Remember, as Abraham departed, this rich Black king gave Abraham riches and servants, thus adding to his wealth.

God Uses A Black Pharoah to Help Israel

Our next stop finds the great grandson of Abraham, Jacob, who is the bearer of the "torch of promise" given to his grandfather. Jacob, whose name was changed by God to Israel, had twelve sons by several wives, thus the term "the twelve tribes of Israel". It was upon Jacob that the promise was now placed and it would be through his seed that the promise of God to Abraham would be fulfilled. Let's focus in on Jacob, at a point in time where he and his family were threatened with extinction due to the famine in the land.

It was at this time that Jacob sent his sons to Egypt to buy grain and supplies from the brilliant prime minister of Egypt. There in Egypt, the sons discover that this Prime Minister was none other than their brother, Joseph, whom they had sold into slavery to a caravan of merchants years before. It turned out to be a very happy reunion and a turning point in the future of Israel.

God raised up the Pharaoh in Egypt, a Black man and Joseph's boss, to give to Jacob and all his children the whole of the land of Goshen. Now Jacob's survival and his family's survival during this time of great famine was insured because of the generosity and obedience of the Black Pharaoh. Once again, God raised up a descendant of Ham to rescue His plan for mankind.

"And Joseph placed his father and his brethren, and gave them a possession in the land of Egypt, in the best of the land, in the land of Rameses, as Pharaoh had commanded." Genesis 47:11

God Uses Hobab the Midianite to help Moses

We pick up this story of Moses, the deliverer of Israel, who was cared for and educated in the house of the Black Pharaoh, whose daughter discovered Moses in a basket in the river. We speed through the pages of Biblical history and slow down as we approach Moses after one of the greatest victories in the Bible.

The Egyptian monarch has released the children of Israel to leave Egyptian slavery. They were victorious at the crossing of the Red Sea, they had received the Commandments from God and now they were preparing to journey through the wilderness to the promised land.

Moses was faced with the task of trying to navigate through the wilderness and he solicited the help of Hobab, the son of Jethro the

Midianite. Now the Midianites were a race of Black people who were the offsprings of Abraham and his Black wife Keturah. Remember, previously, how Hobab's sister, Moses' wife, was referred to as an Ethiopian woman.

Obviously, Moses really needed the help of Hobab, because when Hobab initially refused the offer to become a scout and guide, Moses pleaded with Hobab.

"Thus were the journeyings of the children of Israel according to their armies, when they set forward.

And Moses said unto Hobab, the son of Raguel the Midianite, Moses' father in law, We are journeying unto the place of which the Lord said, I will give it you: come thou with us, and we will do thee good: for the Lord hath spoken good concerning Israel.

And he said unto him, I will not go; but I will depart to mine own land, and to my kindred.

And he said, Leave us not, I pray thee; forasmuch as thou knowest how we are to encamp in the wilderness, and thou mayest be to us instead of eyes.

And it shall be, if thou go with us, yea, it shall be, that what goodness the Lord shall do unto us, the same will we do unto thee.

And they departed from the mount of the Lord three days' journey: and the ark of the covenant of the Lord went before them in the three days' journey, to search out a resting place for them." Numbers 10:28-33

Hobab accepted the offer and became a part of the non-Israelite group who traveled with Moses through the wilderness and ultimately into the promised land. Hobab's descendants received their promised portion in the promised land in Judges 4:11, 1:16 (as Moses had promised).

"And the children of the Kenite, Moses' father in law, went up out of the city of palm trees with the children of Judah into the wilderness of Judah, which lieth in the south of Arad; and they went and dwelt among the people. Judges 1:16

Now Heber the Kenite, which was of the children of Hobab the father in law of Moses, has severed himself from the Kenites, and pitched his tent unto the plain of Zaanaim, which is by Kedesh." Judges 4:11

It was this Black man who assisted Moses and

the children of Israel in their journey through the wilderness at a very critical time in their history. Again, God's strategic use of a person of color to rescue His plan for mankind is clearly seen.

Both Joshua and Caleb were Descendants of Black People

I know that this will probably be a very shocking revelation that the two spies who returned from viewing the promised land and gave a good report were most likely people of color. Don't lose sight that the issue we are discussing is the issue of color. We have discovered that the people of color were derived either directly or indirectly (through intermarrying) from the Black man Ham and his descendants.

Was Caleb Black?

It is assumed that Caleb was a member of one of the tribes of Israel because he represented one of them when men were chosen to spy out the promised land. Simple study of scripture proves that Caleb was a Kenezite and not an Israelite.

"Then the children of Judah came unto Joshua in Gilgal: and Caleb the son of Jephunneh the Kenezite said unto him, Thou knowest the thing that the Lord said unto Moses the man of God

concerning me and thee in Kadesh-barnea.

Hebron therefore became the inheritance of Caleb the son of Jephunneh the Kenezite unto this day, because that he wholly followed the Lord God of Israel." Joshua 14:6,14

This scripture shows that Caleb was the son of Jephunneh the Kenezite. The Kenezites and the Kenites were related to the Midianites, who were descendants of Black people. Careful reading of the dividing-up of the promised land shows that Caleb received his portion within the tribe of Judah in Hebron.

"And Joshua blessed him, and gave unto Caleb the son of Jephunneh Hebron for an inheritance.

Hebron therefore became the inheritance of Caleb the son of Jephunneh the Kenezite unto this day, because that he wholly followed the Lord God of Israel." Joshua 14:13-14

"And unto Caleb the son of Jephunneh he gave a part among the children of Judah, according to the commandment of the Lord to Joshua, even the city of Arba the father of Anak, which city is Hebron.

And Caleb drove thence the three sons of Anak,

Sheshai, and Ahiman, and Talmai, the children of Anak." Joshua 15:13-14

Was Joshua a man of color?

Of all that we have heard about Joshua it has never been mentioned that he was a descendant from one of the Black tribes of Israel. In a previous chapter we discovered through the scripture that Jacob adopted the sons of Joseph, Manassah and Ephraim, by his Black Egyptian wife. This would make these people of the tribes of Ephraim and Manassah people of color. Joshua was from the tribe of Ephraim.

"Of the children of Joseph: of Ephraim; Elishama the son of Ammihud: of Manasseh; Gamaliel the son of Pedahzur." Numbers 1:10

"Of the tribe of Ephraim, Oshea (Joshua) the son of Nun.

These are the names of the men which Moses sent to spy out the land. And Moses called Oshea (Joshua) the son of Nun Jehoshua." Numbers 13:8, 16

I believe it is safe to conclude that Joshua was a man of color, a descendant of Joseph and his Egyptian wife, Asenath.

These two men of color, Joshua and Caleb, viewed the promised land and returned with the bold faith report that kept Israel on track with God's plan. It was their report and faith in the faithfulness of God that guaranteed a remnant of the nation possessing the promised land. Ten of the spies who returned with an evil report of fear negatively persuaded the hearts of the adult population. They implied that God had forsaken them and that they would be destroyed and would not survive in the promised land. The plan of God was rescued and preserved alive for the next generation and carried out because of the courage and boldness of these two men of color.

The Black Woman Who Helped Save a Nation

Rahab the harlot is always looked upon with such shame because of her profession that other factors about her life are overlooked. The Bible records her as a harlot in Jericho, during the time when Israel was about to take possession of the promised land. You must remember now, Jericho was a city in Canaan, that was inhabited by Black people who were descendants of the Black man Ham. This would make Rahab a "Black" Canaanite woman!

Her assistance was critical in the overthrow of

the walled city of Jericho. Joshua had sent spies to search out the city of Jericho. They were discovered and were assisted by this Black woman in Joshua 2:1-4. The spies returned with critical strategical information about Jericho that assisted in the victory.

Because she later helped them escape, she was rewarded when the city was overthrown. The warriors of Israel were instructed to be sure to spare her and her house. She was allowed to become a part of their nation. She traveled with them and later married among them, and became a part of the lineage of Jesus.

"Now therefore, I pray you, swear unto me by the Lord, since I have shewed you kindness, that ye will also shew kindness unto my father's house, and give me a true token:

And that ye will save alive my father, and my mother, and my brethren, and my sisters, and all that they have, and deliver our lives from death.

And the men answered her, Our life for yours, if ye utter not this our business. And it shall be, when the Lord hath given us the land, that we will deal kindly and truly with thee.

Then she let them down by a cord through the

window: for her house was upon the town wall, and she dwelt upon the wall.

And she said unto them, Get you to the mountain, lest the pursuers meet you; and hide yourselves there three days, until the pursuers be returned: and afterward may ye go your way.

And the men said unto her, We will be blameless of this thine oath which thou hast made us swear.

Behold, when we come into the land, thou shalt bind this line of scarlet thread in the window which thou didst let us down by: and thou shalt bring thy father, and thy mother, and thy brethren, and all thy father's household, home unto thee." Joshua 2:12-18

Here again one of Ham's descendants is strategically used to assist in the success of the plan of God. You must agree that this victory was critical because it set the stage for the future battles in Canaan. Rahab's influence doesn't stop here because as we have shown in previous chapters, she was in the lineage of Jesus. It is clear to see that, obviously, being Black does not exclude one from participation in the plan of God.

The Black Phillistine Army that Helped David

"And all his servants passed on beside him; and all the Cherethites, and all the Pelethites, and all the Gittites, six hundred men which came after him from Gath, passed on before the king." II Samuel 15:18

The scene in the above text finds David at a very low ebb in his reign in Israel. His son, Absolam, has treacherously engineered a revolt and has taken the throne from his father. David is now on the run and only the extremely loyal and committed followers are with him.

There is among these followers a fearless band of Black men from Gath led by Ittai. Gath was one of the five cities of the Philistines, whose inhabitants were called Gittites.

"From Sihor, which is before Egypt, even unto the borders of Ekron northward, which is counted to the Canaanite: five lords of the Philistines; the Gazathites, and the Ashdothites, the Eshkalonites, the Gittites, and the Ekronites; also the Avites:" Joshua 13:3

The Philistines were descendants of the Black man Ham, through his son Mizraim (Egypt).

These six hundred men were committed to King David in a time of crisis and were instrumental in helping David regain his throne. You probably never heard the story of these six hundred brave men who helped get the plan of God back on track after a serious derailment. I don't believe that it is coincidental that these men were positioned as they were. It shows God's conspicuous use of Ham's descendants again.

The Black Man Who Rescued Jeremiah From Death

Almost every student of the Old Testament will recognize the name of Jeremiah the prophet. He was instrumental in giving many powerful and important prophecies to his people for their day and our day. The text shows Jeremiah in a life-threatening situation. His bold prophecies were not received well by everyone.

"Thus saith the Lord, He that remaineth in this city shall die by the sword, by the famine, and by the pestilence: but he that goeth forth to the Chaldeans shall live; for he shall have his life for a prey, and shall live.

Thus saith the Lord, This city shall surely be given into the hand of the king of Babylon's army, which shall take it.

Therefore the princes said unto the king, We beseech thee, let this man be put to death: for thus he weakeneth the hands of the men of war that remain in this city, and the hands of all the people, in speaking such words unto them: for this man seeketh not the welfare of this people, but the hurt.

Then Zedekiah the king said, Behold, he is in your hand: for the king is not he that can do any thing against you.

Then took they Jeremiah, and cast him into the dungeon of Malchiah the son of Hammelech, that was in the court of the prison: and they let down Jeremiah with cords. And in the dungeon there was no water, but mire: so Jeremiah sunk in the mire.

Now when Ebed-melech the Ethiopian, one of the eunuchs which was in the king's house, heard that they had put Jeremiah in the dungeon; the king then sitting in the gate of Benjamin;

Ebed-melech went forth out of the king's house, and spake to the king, saying,

My lord the king, these men have done evil in all

that they have done to Jeremiah the prophet, whom they have cast into the dungeon; and he is like to die for hunger in the place where he is: for there is no more bread in the city.

Then the king commanded Ebed-melech the Ethiopian, saying, Take from hence thirty men with thee, and take up Jeremiah the prophet out of the dungeon, before he die.

So Ebed-melech took the men with him, and went into the house of the king under the treasury, and took thence old cast clouts and old rotten rags, and let them down by cords into the dungeon to Jeremiah.

And Ebed-melech the Ethiopian said unto Jeremiah, Put now these old cast clouts and rotten rags under thine armholes under the cords. And Jeremiah did so.

So they drew up Jeremiah with cords, and took him up out of the dungeon: and Jeremiah remained in the court of the prison.

Then Zedekiah the king sent, and took Jeremiah the prophet unto him into the third entry that is in the house of the Lord: and the king said unto Jeremiah, I will ask thee a thing; hide nothing from me.

Then Jeremiah said unto Zedekiah, If I declare it unto thee, wilt thou not surely put me to death? and if I give thee counsel, wilt thou not hearken unto me?" Jeremiah 38:2-15

On this occasion Jeremiah's words were rejected by the Captain of the guard, because he foretells the coming destruction and capture of the city. Jeremiah even tells King Zedekiah that he will be killed by the king of Babylon. Such prophecy was most unpopular and was viewed as a threat to the morale of the fighting army.

Jeremiah was thrown in the dungeon which was filled with mire, (thick mud), without food or water. Jeremiah's death was imminent, except that God raised up Ebedmelech, the Ethiopian, to rescue him. By now, it should be getting clearer that God seems to use people of color to rescue his people and his plan.

Elijah Depends on the Black Woman to Sustain Him

"And the word of the Lord came unto him, saying,

Arise, get thee to Zarephath, which belongeth to Zidon, and dwell there: behold, I have commanded a widow woman there to sustain thee.

So he arose and went to Zarephath. And when he came to the gate of the city, behold, the widow woman was there gathering of sticks: and he called to her, and said, Fetch me, I pray thee, a little water in a vessel, that I may drink.

And as she was going to fetch it, he called to her, and said, Bring me, I pray thee, a morsel of bread in thine hand.

And she said, As the Lord thy God liveth, I have not a cake, but an handful of meal in a barrel, and a little oil in a cruse: and, behold, I am gathering two sticks, that I may go in and dress it for me and my son, that we may eat it, and die.

And Elijah said unto her, Fear not; go and do as thou hast said: but make me thereof a little cake first, and bring it unto me, and after make for thee and for thy son.

For thus saith the Lord God of Israel, The barrel of meal shall not waste, neither shall the cruse of oil fail, until the day that the Lord sendeth rain upon the earth.

And she went and did according to the saying of

Elijah: and she, and he, and her house, did eat many days.

And the barrel of meal wasted not, neither did the cruse of oil fail, according to the word of the Lord, which he spake by Elijah." I Kings 17:8-16

This is a familiar story but look at verse nine and note where Zarephath is.

"Arise, get thee to Zarephath, which belongeth to Zidon, and dwell there: behold, I have commanded a widow woman there to sustain thee." I Kings 17:9

The verse says that it belongs to Zidon. Zidon and Sidon are different names to reference the same place. When Jesus was in His earthly ministry, he mentioned this story of Elijah and the widow and he called the place Sidon.

"But unto none of them was Elias sent, save unto Sarepta, a city of Sidon, unto a woman that was a widow." Luke 4:26

Sidon was the firstborn son of Canaan, the son of the Black man, Ham.

"And Canaan begat Sidon his firstborn, and

Heth," Genesis 10:15

Sidon was the city founded and inhabited by these descendants of Ham. This woman was of Sidonian heritage, and was therefore a descendant of the Black man Ham through Canaan.

The story of the text is quite clear, Elijah was waiting as he was instructed by God to do by the brook Cherith. The brook dried up because of the lack of rain, and Elijah was in serious trouble. God instructed him that a widow will sustain him in Zarephath, a city of Sidon.

This obedient widow whose name is never mentioned was faithful to obey God and received her miracle that blessed both her and the prophet. God used her to sustain the prophet as he was in preparation for his greatest battle with the false prophets of Baal. Once again a black-skinned person was used by God to play a very pivotal role in sustaining His plan!

Joseph hides Jesus in Black Egypt

"And when they were come into the house, they saw the young child with Mary his mother, and fell down, and worshipped him: and when they had opened their treasures, they presented unto

him gifts; gold, and frankincense, and myrrh.

And being warned of God in a dream that they should not return to Herod, they departed into their own country another way.

And when they were departed, behold, the angel of the Lord appeareth to Joseph in a dream, saying, Arise, and take the young child and his mother, and flee into Egypt, and be thou there until I bring thee word: for Herod will seek the young child to destroy him.

When he arose, he took the young child and his mother by night, and departed into Egypt:

And was there until the death of Herod: that it might be fulfilled which was spoken of the Lord by the prophet, saying, Out of Egypt have I called my son.

Then Herod, when he saw that he was mocked of the wise men, was exceeding wroth, and sent forth, and slew all the children that were in Bethlehem, and in all the coasts thereof, from two years old and under, according to the time which he had diligently inquired of the wise men.

Then was fulfilled that which was spoken by Jeremy the prophet, saying,

In Rama was there a voice heard, lamentation, and weeping, and great mourning, Rachel weeping for her children, and would not be comforted, because they are not." Matthew 2:11-18

The story of the birth of Jesus has probably been read by most Christians at one time or another. The text shows that Herod sought to kill the Christ child and sent men to search throughout the land to find him. In a dream Joseph was instructed to escape and hide in Egypt with Jesus and his mother.

It is amazing that God told Joseph that Jesus would find safe haven in the land of Egypt. Of course we know that Egypt is the land of the descendants of the Black man Ham. Again Ham's descendants were playing an important role in the plan of God. Needless to remind you again that Jesus was probably a man of color, thus easy to hide among other Black children.

The Church at Antioch With Black Leadership Becomes the Model

Although the church experienced tremendous growth in the early years of its existence, it also experienced tremendous persecution. The persecution was so great that the disciples were scattered abroad. Certain disciples went to Antioch and established a local church that became pivotal to the evangelization of the world.

"And some of them were men of Cyprus and Cyrene, which, when they were come to Antioch, spake unto the Grecians, preaching the Lord Jesus.

And when he had found him, he brought him unto Antioch. And it came to pass, that a whole year they assembled themselves with the church, and taught much people. And the disciples were called Christians first in Antioch." Acts 11:20,26

"Now there were in the church that was at Antioch certain prophets and teachers; as Barnabas, and Simeon that was called Niger, and Lucius of Cyrene, and Manaen, which had been brought up with Herod the tetrarch, and Saul.

As they ministered to the Lord, and fasted, the Holy Ghost said, Separate me Barnabas and Saul for the work whereunto I have called them.

And when they had fasted and prayed, and laid

their hands on them, they sent them away." Acts 13:1-3

There are several people of color that I want you to notice in this missionary-minded church. Note, Simeon called Niger, the word "Niger" means Black. Lucius of Cyrene was also a Black man. Cyrenians were Black. Of course, you remember Simon the Cyrenian who bore the cross of Jesus. Cyrene was a capital district of Cyrenaica in Africa. Cyrene was represented in Jerusalem (with the disciples) on the day of Pentecost.

"Phrygia, and Pamphylia, in Egypt, and in the parts of Libya about Cyrene, and strangers of Rome, Jews and proselytes," Acts 2:10

After the dispersion of the disciple from Jerusalem, these bold Black men founded the church at Antioch. The scripture exposes the importance of this church as it became a model for other churches. The disciples were first called Christians at Antioch. It was from this church that the Apostle Paul was sent forth on his missionary journeys and returned periodically to report on His work. The most notable New Testament Apostle submitted himself to the Black leadership at the church at Antioch.

Further study also reveals the close relationship that Paul had with Simon of Cyrene. Simon had two sons, Rufus and Alexander, whose mother he refers to in an endearing way.

"And they compel one Simon a Cyrenian, who passed by, coming out of the country, the father of Alexander and Rufus, to bear his cross." Mark 15:21

Later, Paul refers to Rufus, Simon's son, in his letter to the church at Rome.

"Salute Rufus chosen in the Lord, and his mother and mine." Romans 16:13

The Apostle Paul refers to Rufus's mother as being like his very own mother. Out of all that you have heard about the Apostle Paul, it has never been said that he felt a close kindred to these Black disciples at Antioch.

When the new testament church was facing extinction and annihilation from its persecutors, these brave disciples forged ahead and structured the first "Christian Missionary Church". Once again here is proof of God's use of people of color to carry out critical assignments that affected His plan for mankind.

The Redemption Plan is Helped by a Black Man

"And they were instant with loud voices, requiring that he might be crucified. And the voices of them and of the chief priests prevailed.

And Pilate gave sentence that it should be as they required.

And he released unto them him that for sedition and murder was cast into prison, whom they had desired; but he delivered Jesus to their will.

And as they led him away, they laid hold upon one Simon, a Cyrenian, coming out of the country, and on him they laid the cross, that he might bear it after Jesus.

And there followed him a great company of people, and of women, which also bewailed and lamented him." Luke 23:23-27

I doubt that anyone will argue about the importance of the death and resurrection of Jesus Christ. The importance of Calvary is critical in that the manner of his death had been prophesied and had to happen as it was foretold without a hitch. If Jesus had died during the awful beating or on the way to Golgatha, it would not have been the same.

Get the picture now. Jesus was bleeding from the beating with the whip that was called the **"cat of nine tails"**. This beating literally tore away flesh from the bone. The crown of thorns had been crushed into his skull, and blood was gushing from the wounds. They laid a cross upon him and were leading him to the place of execution. Jesus was already close to death as he fell under the weight of the cross, with no strength to make the journey up the hill of Golgatha.

God strategically positioned a Black man, Simon of Cyrene, to help Jesus bear the cross and assist in the fulfillment of God's plan for mankind. Think of it. A Black man picked up the cross that was wet with the actual blood of Jesus. It is safe to say that this Black man was the first recorded man touched by the blood of Jesus.

Has God Chosen Black People for a Purpose?

No one doubts that the Bible has recorded that God has chosen Israel for a special purpose, but is Israel the only group of people chosen for a purpose? Absolutely Not! Look at this scripture in Isaiah 43:3-4:

"For I am the Lord thy God, the Holy One of Israel, thy Savior: I gave Egypt for thy ransom,

Ethiopia and Seba for thee." Isaiah 43:3

To understand this message of the prophet Isaiah, you must understand what a ransom is. A ransom is a tool or a thing that is used to initiate a positive outcome of a life-threatening situation. When a person or thing has been kidnapped, his capturers will normally request a **"ransom"** in exchange for the person's or thing's freedom.

The importance of the ransom is immeasurable, in that the absence of a proper ransom will result in an undesirable outcome. Jesus was chosen to be the ransom for the world, so that God's plan to save mankind would come to pass.

"But so shall it not be among you: but whosoever will be great among you, shall be your minister:

And whosoever of you will be the chiefest, shall be servant of all.

For even the Son of man came not to be ministered unto, but to minister, and to give his life a ransom for many." Mark 10:43-45

A ransom is a thing that is used to achieve a desirable outcome to what could be a life-threatening situation. In Isaiah, the scripture records that God chose to use Egypt's descendants, Ethoipia's and Seba's children as a ransom, as instruments of positive change in His plan for mankind. As I have shown since the beginning of this chapter, God has strategically used people of color, who are descendants of these Black people to help Israel in times of crisis.

The precept is clear and the examples are many. Therefore, it is undisputable that God has purposely chosen these Black people to be catalysts for positive and constructive change in critical situations.

This is why I believe that each time the plan of God suffered a serious threat, God positioned one of these children of the Black man Ham to rescue it or to assist in the management of a crisis.

If this truth is told, it will dispel the lie that the Black man is inferior and only a spectator in the plan of God. He is everything but a spectator in God's redemptive plan. In fact, the Black man has been and will always be an intricate part of the plan of God.

Maybe that is why the devil has attacked the Black people and Israel, because of their importance to God's plan to redeem all of mankind. Maybe Satan has seen over the years that when the plan of God is in trouble and Israel is threatened that God always seems to raise up a Black man to become the instrument of deliverance and change! Praise God for Purpose!

CHAPTER VII

What America Owes the Black People

CHAPTER VII
What America Owes the Black People

God's strategic use of people of color, who are descendants of the Black man, Ham, destroys several misconceptions about people of color in this society. The truth must be told. First, the color of skin does not make a person inferior to others with a different heritage or color of skin. Second, the color of skin is not an indication of a negative character flaw. Thirdly, that the worth or value of a person to God and to others is not predicated on the color of skin or heritage. Finally, the color of skin is not a sign of potential disloyalty or anti-social behavior.

Since the church is the salt of the earth and the light of the world, we must become a visible example to this society of true racial equality. There are several qualities in salt. One quality is its ability to create a thirst. As this society sees a visible testimony of the character of God amidst his people, there will be a desire to emulate that behavior.

Racial Controversy - Matter of Collaboration?

I was given a copy of a speech reportedly made by a Willie Lynch to a group of slave owners in Virginia. It appears from the speech that Mr.

Lynch was a successful slave owner in the West Indies who was brought in as a consultant to the American slave owners. He instructed them in this speech on successful slave control through the exploitation of differences among the slaves. Mr. Lynch suggested that if these manipulative tactics were properly used, they would indoctrinate the slaves and their future generations and lock them into a permanent, "inferior" mental attitude.

Read carefully the following speech and think about what is actually happening in America. It may be that this is not all just a coincidence but a ripe, age-old conspiracy.

THE SPEECH
By Willie Lynch

Gentlemen:

I greet you here on the banks of the James River in the year of our Lord, one thousand seven hundred and twelve. First, I shall thank you, the Gentlemen of the Colony of Virginia for bringing me here. I am here to help you solve your problems with the slaves. Your invitation reached me on my modest plantation in the West Indies where I have experimented with some of the newest and still the oldest methods for control of slaves. Ancient Rome would envy us if my program is implemented. As our boat sailed south on the James River, named for our illustrious King, whose version of the Bible we cherish, I saw enough to know that your problem is not unique. While Rome used cords of wood as crosses for standing human bodies along its old highways in great numbers, you are here using the tree and rope on occasion.

I caught whiff of a dead slave hanging from a tree a couple of miles back. You are not only losing valuable stock by hangings, you are having uprisings, slaves are running away, your crops are sometimes left in the field too long for maximum profit, you suffer occasional fires, your animals are killed. Gentlemen, you know what your problems are; I do not need to elaborate. I am not here to enumerate your problems, I am here to introduce you to a method of solving them.

In my bag here, I have a fool-proof method for controlling your Black slaves. I guarantee everyone of you that if installed correctly it will control the slaves for at least 300 years. My method is simple and members of your family or any overseer can use it.

I have outlined a number of differences among

the slaves; and I take these differences and make them bigger. I use fear, distrust, and envy for control purposes. These methods have worked on my modest plantation in the West Indies and it will work throughout the South. Take this simple little list of differences, think about them. On top of my list is "age", but it is there only because it starts with an "a"; the second is "color (or shade)"; there is intelligence, size, sex, size of plantation, status on plantation, attitude of owner, whether the slaves live in the valley or on a hill, east, west, north, south, have fine hair or coarse hair, or is tall or short. Now that you have a list of differences, I shall give you an outline of action, but before that, I shall assure you that distrust is stronger than trust, and envy is stronger than adulation, respect or admiration.

The Black slave after receiving this indoctrination shall carry on and will become self-refuelling and self-generating for hundreds of years, maybe thousands.

Don't forget you must pitch the old Black vs. the young Black male and the young Black male vs. the old Black male. You must use the dark skin slaves vs. the light skin slaves and the light skin slaves vs. the dark skin slaves. You must also have your white servants and overseers distrust

ALL blacks, but it is necessary they trust and depend on us. They must love, respect, and trust ONLY us.

Gentlemen, these kits are your control; use them. Have your wives and children use them, never miss an opportunity. My plan is guaranteed, and the good thing about this plan is that if used INTENSELY for one year the slaves themselves will remain perpetually distrustful.

Thank you gentlemen.

Willie Lynch, 1712

Although my efforts to unquestionably validate the absolute authenticity of this speech and the exact time and place it was delivered are not complete at the printing of this book, the contents of this speech cannot go unnoticed. There is an attitude of envy and distrust among Black people in America that is too deeply entrenched to be coincidental. There is also an attitude of superiority that white America seems to have generation after generation that cannot be a matter of chance. Obviously, something is being done to develop these attitudes in these two groups of people generation after generation.

Although we are hundreds of years removed from chattel slavery, there still exists damaging vestiges of a slavery attitude in our country. For a time during the 80's America was anesthetized into thinking that the problem had been solved, certain doors of opportunity opened, and a message of racial equality was the order of the day. The problem of prejudice did not go away. It was simply covered up, but the attitudes and basic beliefs about the worth of people and personal self-worth did not change.

Now, here in the 90's racial unrest is at an all-time high because the cause of racism was never addressed. Until the belief system changes, attitudes and behavior will not be permanently changed. An attitude change goes beyond lip service, slogans, and political rhetoric.

You and I must agree that the previously mentioned "Willie Lynch" tactics have worked successfully. Most whites still have a prejudicial, superior attitude toward Blacks. Some of the poorest of white people possess a sense of superiority over the richest of Black people. The reason is that comparative worth in this society is not based primarily on possessions, skills, and character, but on the color of skin. After that, the other factors come into play.

Each time I hear a white person attempting to prove their lack of prejudice by saying, "But I don't see color," it is an indication that this person is in a state of "denial". Think about it. To say I don't see color is to imply that there is something wrong with color. If there is something so wrong with color that I have to overlook it, this implies that people of color lack worth as they are and therefore their color must be ignored.

Many Black people suffer from prejudicial attitudes that cause them to distrust each other and to feel inferior around white people.

It is appalling that Black businesses fail to succeed in their own neighborhood, failing due to lack of patronage by their own people. There is a deep-seated prejudicial attitude against whites that gives birth to hatred of whites and rejection of authority (since authority is seen as a white man's tool of oppression). The other side of this attitude that Blacks are inferior gives birth to lack of respect for a Black man's life, thus a reason for Black-on-Black homicide.

Until the racist, prejudiced attitude that is inbred in us all in the very early stages of our innocence is dealt with, there will never be an attitude change. Like the alcoholic who denies he has a problem, like the marriage partners who ignore that they have a problem, the racist in denial, both Black and white, will never change, and the solicitation of help is unlikely.

"And be not conformed to this world: but be ye transformed by the renewing of your mind, that ye may prove what is that good, and acceptable, and perfect, will of God." Romans 12:2

The church world must make a break from the predominantly racist attitude of this society and be transformed by seeing all men, in particular Black men, from God's perspective. Both Black and white Christians must make a conscious effort to overcome the misconceptions about each other that have become part of our subconscious. These misconceptions and prejudices are a part of our upbringing, the product of our environment. Remember that when a person is born again his or her character is not immediately changed, but change in character and behavior takes place through purposeful effort.

Ministers and Clergymen must become aggressive in correcting the misinformation that the church world has propagated throughout the nation. They should inform their members and constituents about the role people of color play in the scripture. This truth will cast light on the foregone lies about the character and behavior of people of color and will provoke believers to address certain traditional attitudes.

When the prejudicial attitudes of people are properly dealt with, the individual attitudes that are passed on to the next generation will be changed. The laboratory for change is not the school or the church, but the real laboratory for change is the home. Most of the basic attitudes you formed about life were influenced by impressions that were made on you at home.

The average Black man first hears the word "nigger" from someone he knows within the sphere of his home life. If Black men and women don't want other races of people to call them "niggers", they must eliminate that word from the vocabulary they use at home.

Most whites get their sense of racial superiority from those in the sphere of their home environment. Everybody has the right to have certain preferences or prejudices. This is a simple fact of life. A prejudicial attitude of superiority is detrimental when it causes a person to penalize others, especially when other people don't meet a certain defined skin color criteria.

It is difficult for this generation of whites in America to understand its responsibilities for the past mistreatment of Black people in this country. The whole issue of reverse discrimination is spawned by an attitude of denial of responsibility for what this country has done to inhumanly penalize a people who were brought to this land against their will. Much of the prosperity that this nation enjoys was achieved at the expense of the cheap slave labor and the blood of Black people.

The debt for the forced investment the Black slaves made to the prosperity of this country must be properly paid, with dividends for proper restitution in this generation. Defining what these restitutions are is the real point of discussion. What does America owe the Black People?

The Debt To Be Paid

There is a question that is always addressed to Black leadership from white America. What do you want? What is proper restitution for an act of slavery that was committed years ago by the ancestors of white America? It astounds me that most of the Black leadership is unable to properly address the issue of restitution. The most important factor is often eliminated when Black leadership attempts to answer the question.

Government assistance programs and incentives are important and by all means should never be overlooked as a component of proper restitution.

Other nationalities receive government assistance to insure proper and equal access to the doors of opportunity in this country. I strongly support educational incentives, minority business programs and other low income incentives as a part of the solution. However, economic assistance alone is not proper restitution, in that more than an economic opportunity has been denied.

The period of slavery affected the psychological attitude of the nation toward people of color, as well as the psychological attitude of the people oppressed. Until the propaganda and stereotypes of the slavery era are sufficiently dealt with, there will not be a climate of cooperation and respect among the races of people in this society. The dignity and self-worth of Black people were severely affected by the imposed mindset of slavery. Dignity and self-worth are key elements that are necessary to achieve success in the most favorable societies.

America owes the Black people in this country assistance in the restoration of their dignity and respect and the elimination of all propaganda to the contrary. This can be achieved through a national media campaign to undo what the post-slavery media has done to taint the image and character of people of color. This media campaign could be either sponsored by the government or subsidized by the government incentives in the private sector. The sole object of this media campaign would be to change the thinking of people about people of color.

The attitude of Americans has been severely impacted by the national ad campaigns addressing smoking, drinking and other diseases. This is a realistic debt that can be paid in this generation!

The Christian world must take the lead in this effort to use the media to dispel the lies about people of color that have so crippled this society. Black Christians must lead the way in getting the knowledge of who they are from God's perspective and teach the Bible uncompromisingly, declaring the role Black people have played in the plan of God.

This information from the Word of God can dispel the lies that have held people captive. The only way to eliminate the mental stronghold that misinformation causes in our thinking is to expose people to truth. With the truth from the Word of God the believer, whether Black or white, can perform the spiritual principles of II Corinthians 10:5. This is knowledge that every believer needs to know and every believer needs to share with others!

"Casting down imaginations, and every high thing that exalteth itself against the knowledge of God, and bringing into captivity every thought to the obedience of Christ." II Corinthians 10:5

Because you have been exposed to this knoweldge, whose text is the undeniable Word of God, you have the opportunity to live free of the influences of the racist propaganda of this world.

"And ye shall know the truth, and the truth shall make you free." John 8:32

ABOUT THE AUTHOR

Dr. I. V. Hilliard is the multi-gifted Pastor/Teacher of New Light Church and Light Christian Center (One Church, Two Locations), and the Director of Light International Ministries, with headquarters in Houston, Texas.

With a mandate to spread the gospel to his generation, Dr. Hilliard is committed to television and other mass media techniques. His style of ministry and charisma has resulted in thousands hearing the uncompromised Word of God in a refreshing manner.

Along with pastoring and teaching a thriving ministry that is experiencing phenomenal growth, he is the founder of Biblical Success Institute, and Life Change Institute. Dr. Hilliard has authored several books and tapes that minister to the multifarious needs of this generation. The television program" Changing Lives Through Faith" has ministered to cities across America.

Not only is he a man of faith, he is also the father of four lovely daughters. Dr. Hilliard attributes his successes to Almighty God and the inveterate support of his beautiful wife, Bridget.

INDEX

A

Aaron...... 108-109
Abidah......1063108
Abimelech.....86-89, 128, 130-133
Abraham 81-91,106,108, 126-134
Adah.........110,112
Adam...49,51,53-56
Africa.......53,55-56
Ahiman......138,140
Aholibamah.110,112
Alexander...154,156
Ammihud........140
Ammonites......114
Amorite...62,77,129
Anah 112
Anak..........26,139
Antioch......153-154
Apostle Paul.... 68
Asenath.........117
Ashdothites....144
Asshurim.......108
Avites...........144

B

Baal.................151
Babylon............145
Barnabas..........154
Bashemath.........112
Bathsheba............75
Benjamin..78-79,146
Bethlehem........ 152

C

Caleb 119-121,138-139, 140-141,
Canaan 62,73-74,76-77, 80-81
Chaldeans.........145
Cherethites........144
Cherith.............151
Cush.....52,53,55,61, 65,111
Cyprus............154
Cyrene..154-155,158
Cyrenians.........155

INDEX

D
David.. 72, 75, 101, 103
Dedan............108

E
Ebed-melech.. 146-147
Edom..........112-113
Edomites. 113-114, 120
Egyptian... 68-70, 109, 135, 140
Ekron................144
Ekronites............144
Eldaash.............108
Eliezer........110-111
Elijah..........148-151
Eliphaz.............112
Elishama..........140
Elon the Hittite....112
Ephah..............108
Epher................108
Ephraim.. 117-118, 140
Ephrom the Hittite................90
Esau............111-113
Eshkalonites........144
Ethiopia.....53-55, 65, 159-160

E (cont'd)
Ethiopian....110-111, 136, 147
Euphrates..........120

G
Gamaliel...........140
Gath............72, 144
Gazathites..........144
Gershom.....110-111
Gilgal..............138
Girgasite........62, 77
Gittites.............144
Golgatha..........157
Goshen............116

H
Hagar................107
Ham.........21, 52, 55, 63, 82, 89, 91, 100, 111, 133, 141, 143-145, 151, 153, 160, 165
Hammelech........146
Hanroch...........108
Havilah..........51, 52

INDEX

H (cont'd)

Hebron............139
Heli................102
Herod...103-104,152
Heth...........74,151
Hittites......74,77-78
Hivites.........62,79
Hobab.....135-137

I

Ishbak............108
Ishmael..........107

J

Jaalam............112
Jacob..101,111,113, 134,140
Jebusites...62,77-78
Jephnunneh 120,138-139
Jerusalem...77,129, 155
Jeremiah.....145-146
Jethro........110,135
Jeush..............112
Jokshan...........108

J (cont'd)

Joseph.......103,116, 134,140
Joshua.......102-103, 119,138-140,142-143
Judah....120,137,139

K

Kadesh-Barnea..119, 120,139
Kadmonites.......120
Kenezite.....120,139
Kenites......120,137
Kenizzites........120
Keturah's Children..........108
Korah..............112

L

Letushim..........108
Leummim.........108
Libya..............155
Lost Coin..........33

INDEX

L (cont'd)

Lost Sheep.........35
Lost Son........36,38
Lucius (of Cyrene)
.....................154

M

Malchiah........146
Manasseh...117-118, 140
Mary.........103,151
Medan.............108
Melchizedek...83,86, 88,127,129-130
Midian........108-110
Midianite....135-136
Miriam.....68,71,110
Mizraim (Egypt)
.....52-53,61-62,70
Moabites..........114
Moses...69,110-111, 136-138

N

Nebajoth.........112
Nimrod.......61-62, 64-67
Nineveh......62,67
Noah's Children
..................52,61
Nun...............120

O

Obed............102
Oshea(Joshua)..140

P

Pamphylia.......155
Pedahzur........139
Pelethites........144
Perizzites..........79
Pharaoh....110,135
Philistines....71-72, 89,133,144
Phrygia..........155
Pilate............157
Proselytes......155

INDEX

R
Rahab..102-103,141
Rama.............153
Rameses..........135
Rebekah...111-112
Reuel............112
Rufus............156

S
Salem.....77,83-86, 127-128,130
Sarah......88,90-91, 107,131,133
Saul..........71,154
Seba..............159
Seir (mount).....113
Sheba............108
Sheshai..........140
Shuah............108
Sidon..........63,74, 150-151
Sihor.............144
Simeon (the Niger) 154-155
Simon the Canaanite......76
Solomon.65,75,103, 114

T
Talmai.............140

U
Uriah the Hittite 74-75

Z
Zaphnath-paaneah 117
Zarephath...148,149, 151
Zedekiah..........146
Zibeon............112
Zidon.......148,150
Zidonians.........114
Zimran............108
Zipporah.........110

NOTES